UNPLUGGED PLAY

PLAY

GRADE SCHOOL

216 ACTIVITIES & GAMES FOR AGES 6-10

BOBBI CONNER

WORKMAN PUBLISHING * NEW YORK

For Cassidy, Olivia, and Peter

Library of Congress Cataloging-in-Publication Data is available.

ISBN 978-1-5235-1020-7

Design by Rae Ann Spitzenberger

Workman books are available at special discounts when purchased in bulk for premiums and sales promotions as well as for fund-raising or educational use. Special editions or book excerpts can also be created to specification. For details, contact the Special Sales Director at the address below, or send an email to specialmarkets@workman.com.

Workman Publishing Co., Inc.
225 Varick Street
New York, NY 10014-4381
workman.com

WORKMAN is a registered trademark of Workman Publishing Co., Inc.

Printed in China
First printing July 2020

10 9 8 7 6 5 4 3 2 1

CONTENTS

PLAY MATTERS
WHY—AND HOW—I WROTE THIS BOOK

C hildren like to play. And why wouldn't they? It's fun! So it makes sense that the more they play, the more they will want to play again. It's a lovely, self-perpetuating cycle that most parents intuitively understand. But what is harder to grasp is the power of play to shape a child's world, particularly a world that is high-tech, fast paced, and plugged in.

And that's why I wrote this book. During my twenty years as host of the nationally syndicated *Parent's Journal* public radio show, I've chatted with many of the leaders in the world of child development. Whether it was David Elkind or Penelope Leach, Fred Rogers or Benjamin Spock, they all—every one of them—spoke of the significance of play. And now I want to help parents help their children enjoy the wholesome, old-fashioned experience of playing creatively and freely . . . *without technology*. I started by collecting and inventing hundreds of games, and then I tested them one by one on different groups of children, ages twelve months to ten years. When the kids rejected a game or an activity, I rejected it too. When a game inspired them to come up with a variation of their own, I appropriated their invention. The result is the more than two hundred "unplugged" games that you have here.

But why "unplugged," you may ask. Since most of us embrace technology to some extent every day—can you imagine a world without email?—it may seem far-fetched to suggest that parents minimize the amount of time their child spends connected to anything with a screen, a plug, or a battery. Besides, it's so easy to plunk a kid in front of a screen! But children need to interact with living, breathing human playmates, and not be held captive by the lights, sounds, and images on a screen. They need to run, chase, ride, skip, and jump, and not *sit still* for prolonged blocks of time. We need only look at the huge rise in childhood obesity to understand how children suffer physically when they remain inactive.

But the toll on kids who rely primarily on electronics for their entertainment goes way beyond some extra pounds. When a child sits in front of a screen, he has no opportunity to connect with the natural world—mud, water, sand, stones, leaves, seeds, animals, insects, sunshine, and rain. It might not seem like such a huge loss in the moment when your child is contentedly clicking buttons on the keypad, but there is something essential about a child getting his hands messy. In addition, because electronic games are preprogrammed with finite possible responses, they limit the imagination. A child who draws, paints, builds, and invents knows a creativity that has no boundaries. By learning that she has the ability to shape her world—either alone or in the company of others—she gains the self-confidence she needs to grow into a problem-solving, creative adult.

And who could ask for more?

—*Bobbi Conner*

THE
POWER
OF PLAY

You may feel as though life has changed in an essential way, and that there is no time for the kind of old-fashioned, wholesome, playful childhood that you had envisioned for your child. But there are the same twenty-four hours in each day and the same seven days in each week. What's changed is the pace of life.

To a large extent, you, as the parent, are the keeper of the time in your family. You arrange the family schedule; you set dinnertime, bath time, and bedtime; and you get your child to appointments, childcare, playgroups, and school *on time*. As the keeper of the time, you have the power and authority to slow time down. And if you make that choice, you'll probably find that your child has more time for all sorts of unplugged play.

Let me give you an example from my own life as a mom. When my son was in kindergarten and my daughter was three, I worked full-time. I was a single parent earning a living for our family of three by day and doing all the typical parenting tasks by night. I always felt rushed. I picked my children up from their Montessori school each day at 5:00 P.M. and headed home. The moment I walked in the door I jumped right into making dinner. (And in the back of my mind I was thinking about the time needed for baths, bedtime stories, and laundry too.) So I scurried around the kitchen while the children played on their own. Or at least that's what they were supposed to do. Often, after just a minute or two, a sibling squabble would set off a group meltdown.

This went on for several days in a row that first week of school, and I realized something needed to change. The next day I put a happier plan in place. I walked in the house and said to my children, "Let's get a snack and read a story together!" (I meant now, not later tonight.) We grabbed three apples from the fruit bowl and a small plate of sliced cheese. We went into the living room, snuggled up on the couch, and ate our snack while I began to read *Caps for Sale*. It was a nourishing, calming time, and after fifteen minutes my son said, "I want to play with my LEGOs now." My daughter said, "Me too." Off they went. I started dinner knowing everyone was happy and reconnected. We all had the time and attention we needed to make a graceful transition into our evening together as a family. Our new after-work and after-school routine made an immediate, positive difference in our lives over the years. I often recalled how I had *slowed down time* and applied this same smart thinking whenever our routine and mood felt off-kilter.

> Play is not trivial. When children play, they're doing important work."
>
> **—Fred Rogers**
> Emmy Award–winning creator and host of *Mister Rogers' Neighborhood*

I mention this lesson from my own life for three reasons. One, to assure you that simple solutions are often best for fixing family routines that are out of sync. Two, to encourage you to stop, take a breath, and make whatever changes are necessary to diminish that anxious feeling that comes when time closes in on you. And finally, to remind you that *children need time to play*. It was true when *you* were a child and it is just as true for infants, toddlers, preschoolers, and older children today.

DARE TO UNPLUG

Play is fun, which is the primary reason children want to do it. And the more fun children have while they play, the more they want to play again next time. This basic cause-and-effect law keeps children in perpetual motion, in search of more and more fun and more and more play. But the full story about play doesn't end here. Play is also a powerful way for children to experience the world.

Children learn through their everyday play experiences. In fact, play is perhaps the best way for children six to ten to learn about themselves (and their own capabilities), to learn about one another, and to learn how all things work in the world. What's absolutely brilliant about this evolutionary mechanism is that children don't know and don't particularly care about the learning component to their play. For example, when two eight-year-olds use plastic flyswatters to bat a balloon back and forth across the lawn, they don't take notice of the agility, muscles, and hand-eye coordination they are developing. Physical, intellectual, social, and emotional growth are happening as children go about the everyday business of play.

We parents can't be satisfied, however, with knowing that our children are out there playing, either alone or with others. We need to do everything in our power to encourage *unplugged* play—those marvelous, nonelectronic, time-tested games and activities that build strong bodies (climbing, hopping, running, jumping, tossing, catching), expand the mind (guessing, figuring, remembering, numbering, interpreting), spark creativity (inventing, building, wordplay, making jokes, telling stories, drawing, painting, singing songs), and forge friendships.

THE SIMPLE PLEASURES

Play is serious business when it comes to a child's health and development, according to the American Academy of Pediatrics (AAP). The AAP clinical report, *The Power of Play,* explains how and why playing with parents and peers is the key to building thriving brains, bodies, and social bonds. Here are some of the benefits of play:

- ▶ Helps prevent obesity, heart disease, and diabetes
- ▶ Builds strong bones and muscles
- ▶ Improves an overall sense of well-being

- ▶ Improves sleep
- ▶ Burns calories
- ▶ Diffuses stress
- ▶ Boosts self-esteem

Research also shows that play can improve children's ability to plan and organize, get along with others, regulate emotions, and strengthen language and math skills. The AAP recommends that children six years and older get sixty minutes of moderate to vigorous physical activity on most days of the week, along with muscle and bone strengthening activities three days a week.

Here are just a few of the sensations and experiences that come alive through unplugged play. When you read this list, the essential question to ask yourself is: Can a screen or machine bring the same joyful experience into my child's life?

Play for Joy

▸ Feel the sunshine on your face as you kick a ball around the lawn.

▸ Jump, skip, and roll down the hill.

▸ Learn how to do a cartwheel.

▸ Create your own miniature golf course outdoors.

▸ Play beanbag tossing games in the backyard with a Hula-Hoop.

▸ Make your own fingerprint or sponge-print greeting cards.

Play for Intelligence

▸ Create a village with roads, bridges, cars, and buildings using toys and props.

▸ Build a fort (add heavy books to keep the sheets from slipping off the table).

▸ Make up an adventure story about your dog or cat.

▸ Design a castle with secret passageways and hidden rooms.

▸ Create your own puzzles from magazine photos.

Play for Connection

▸ Put on a play with kids in the neighborhood.

▸ Play relay races outdoors with your friends.

▸ Make a giant playhouse out of cardboard boxes with a parent.

▸ Build a puppet stage and put on a puppet show.

▸ Play water-balloon tossing games outdoors with your pals.

Children stretch their attention spans and learn to manage their emotions. They become the masters of their own destiny and directors of their own experience. This is true in the first year of life and every week, month, and year thereafter. Children also learn that they are capable of entertaining and amusing themselves, without machines and without an adult!

Within this broad category of unplugged play, there are many types of games for your child to experience. First up are the loads of clever and creative games a child can play alone—on-the-spot activities that parents can offer whenever they need a few minutes to make dinner, work, or chat on the phone. But teaching kids how to amuse themselves is not some selfish act; rather, showing them that they don't have to reach for a screen whenever a parent or friend is not around is a lifelong gift.

And then, of course, there are tons of games to play with one or two friends, or with large groups (such as at birthday parties or playgroups)—the absolute best way for a child to develop social skills, again, whatever the child's age. This holds true for the shy child, the child who gravitates toward one particular playmate, or the child who thrives in a large group. Play is a magnificent way to learn to get along with others, to take turns, to negotiate; it also teaches children about fairness, making amends, and what it feels like to have a friend. Finally, there are games that parents and children can enjoy together, in the park or at the kitchen table. Bringing an entire family together creates another wonderful tradition of play (see "Family

Game Night," page 249). I've tried to include games that do not require an adult to wear a donkey hat or sing "Yankee Doodle" while standing on one foot. But far be it from me to tell you to put dignity in the way of a good time!

WHAT'S WRONG WITH ELECTRONIC PLAY?

Okay, I can hear you muttering in the background—*What world does she live in?*—so it's time to get real. I am not suggesting that electronic games and high-tech play have no place in a child's world, but I feel very strongly that they should occupy only a minor amount of a child's playtime.

Do you want to know why? I've covered some of these points earlier, but they're worth remembering. To begin with, many children play these games in isolation. So rather than interacting with human playmates, they're being captivated by lights, sounds, and moving images. The ramifications on developing social skills (and friendships) are huge. Furthermore, it's a good bet that your child will not be running around while

 If you've been around kids, particularly young kids, for any length of time, [you know] it's absolutely true that all the most important things in life are learned through play."

—Penelope Leach, PhD
psychologist and author
of *Your Baby and Child*

playing on a screen. (Is it any wonder that we are witnessing a huge rise in childhood obesity?) And it's not just the physical benefits that he'll be missing. When your child draws, paints, builds, and invents, or writes music, songs, poems, and stories, there are no artificial boundaries or predetermined limits to his creativity. And when he's playing outside, there's even more freedom—in the form of mud, water, sand, stones, leaves, seeds, animals, insects, sunshine, rain.

FIGHTING THE FIGHT: NOT GIVING IN TO HIGH-TECH PRESSURE

Given all this, you may be wondering how in the world these technology-based games have become so popular—they're *always* there, and nearly everyone seems to be playing. The short answer has to do with successful advertising. The longer answer includes peer pressure, the mistaken belief among parents and educators that children must learn to be proficient on the computer at age four or five or ten or they will be left in the dust academically, and the fact that playing a video to amuse a child is just easier to do when you need a quiet moment for yourself.

But that's only part of the story. Put a kid in front of a large screen with bright, quick-moving images, and chances are his eyes will light up and he will follow the movement on the screen with intensity. Now add interesting sounds, and your

Most of the television viewing that goes on in under twos is not useful, partly because a television program moves at quite the wrong pace for a baby of eighteen months. He turns his head to call your attention to something on the screen. By the time he turns back, it's gone, it's over."

—Penelope Leach, PhD
psychologist and author of *Your Baby and Child*

child's auditory attention will be fixed on that screen as well. So your child appears to be having fun. That's one thing. The other is that high-tech gadgets are so much a part of our adult lives—and we value them so highly—that we imagine they must be of use to children too. They can be. Children with physical limitations or special needs can really benefit from gadgets and games that allow them to connect to friends. And all children, once they get into school, will need to learn to use computers and tablets and phones. But hold back. Children are not mini adults.

DIBS: A THREE-STEP ACTION PLAN

My best advice is to treat high-tech play like a hot fudge sundae—perfectly fine for now and then, but not for every day. Easy for me to say! And not so easy for you to do. But here's a three-point action plan called DIBS that may help.

1. Delay introducing your child to high-tech toys, computers, and electronic games during the infant, toddler, preschool, and kindergarten years, when your child's brain is growing rapidly and incorporating all the social, emotional, and physical development that goes with that. Educational psychologist Jane Healy, author of *Your Child's Growing Mind*, has studied children's use of computers for years and has concluded that they will *not* be disadvantaged if they are not introduced to computers until age seven or eight.

2. Introduce your child to the habit of having fun without plug-ins. That's what this book is for! Let the pleasure of good old-fashioned play win your child's heart.

EIGHT WAYS TO PROMOTE A NO-BATTERY ZONE

1 Provide toys that allow variety—balls, a sandbox, building blocks, art supplies, etc.

2 Change it up by encouraging all types of play: high-energy and physical play, quiet games, arts, crafts, music, building, and imaginative play. Relax. Unplugged play is fun. Children don't need to know that it's often educational. Look for small windows of opportunity that can flow seamlessly into your day—start a silly guessing game at the dinner table, tell a story in the car on the drive across town. Keep it casual. Keep it short.

3 Make your home a place that other children enjoy visiting. It's easier to control what kinds of games kids play on your own turf.

4 Don't hover, and don't micromanage your child's play. Let him explore matters on his own. Simply offer a quick demo about using a toy or a new material (if needed), and then back off.

5 If your child looks stumped, toss out a play-inducing challenge: "What sort of fort could you make with these boxes and blankets?"

6 Don't be afraid to let grandparents, friends, and gift givers know you prefer low-tech or no-tech toys for your child. And until your child is in school, try to keep her away from high-tech anything.

7 As kids get older, set up a Family Electronic Play Plan. You—not your child—should decide how much time is allowed for electronic play each week, and when to fit it into your routine. Some families limit electronic toys and play to weekends. You'll know best what works for you. (See what the American Academy of Pediatrics recommends to curb electronic play, page 11.)

8 Create a regular time that is Family Game Night—once a month or once a week—and put it on your calendar so you don't forget. (See Family Game Night ideas, page 249.)

3. Be selective and deliberate about how much time you allow for electronic play in your older child's week and which games are okay. Make a specific Electronic Play Plan for your family and stick to it. (See suggestions from other families below.)

MAKE AN ELECTRONIC PLAY PLAN

Time for another reality check: The American Academy of Pediatrics (AAP) says that excessive media use has been associated with obesity, lack of sleep, school problems, aggression, and other behavioral issues. The AAP recommends that parents set limits on daily screen time and decide what types of media are appropriate for their child. But as your child gets older, screen time becomes more difficult to control. That's why it's important to set these boundaries early on.

So, what's a parent to do? Here are some specific plans that other real families have used to limit electronic play and screen time:

▶ Create two distinct bins or boxes for toys—one for electronics and another for all unplugged toys and games—so that you're better able to put time restrictions in place for toys chosen from the electronic toy bin.

▶ Create a reading bank in your family. Encourage your child to read for pleasure. For every thirty minutes of reading time banked during the week, your child can engage in an equal amount of screen time on the weekend.

▶ Consider a no screen time rule during the week for school-age children. On weekends, offer a rich assortment of unplugged play opportunities with family and friends, but also allow your child some freedom to choose electronic play.

▶ Connect chore time with electronic game time for older children who clamor for more (beyond the family limit). The idea is that your child can do household chores for a set amount of time, and then trade in for a certain, fixed amount of screen time. (Parents report that this system, while not for everyone, gives the child the power to decide how much effort he is willing to put into earning video playtime.)

The bottom line is that the most effective way to limit electronic play in the early years is to embrace other sorts of play. As your child moves into the preteen years (typically a time of increased pressure for high-tech play), he will begin to play with more independence. You won't be able to prohibit the electronic play that goes on at friends' houses or the high-tech learning tools he's likely to encounter in school, nor should you; in today's world, many of us need

66

By the time children are seven, there have been enormous changes in the brain. Then, the kids are really able to do very interesting and very important things with a computer."

—Jane M. Healy, PhD
educational psychologist and author of
Your Child's Growing Mind and
*Failure to Connect: How Computers
Affect Our Children's Minds*

some degree of technological aptitude. But if you've laid a groundwork of unplugged play, I can guarantee that your child will be more likely to gravitate toward unplugged games— simply because he knows firsthand the pleasure of creating, doing, and playing without plug-ins.

MAKE YOURS AN UNPLUGGED COMMUNITY

Parents who set limits for their children with electronic toys sometimes feel as though they are swimming upstream. To tackle this problem, find other parents who are also swimming upstream and include them in your social circle. Plan potluck dinners with the parents and playdates with the children (or parent and child play parties). Also, organize informal Unplugged Play Parties for small groups of two to four children, with each family involved taking a turn hosting a playdate at their home once a month. There's no need to make these playdate parties especially elaborate or terribly structured. Just provide a little bit of kid-friendly food and opportunities to play indoors and outdoors.

HOW TO USE THIS BOOK

All the games in this book are intended for ages six to ten. You'll find that the games are organized by situation. Who's playing? Just your child? Look in the "Solo" games. You and your child? Flip to "Parent & Child." For two to four children, check out the "Play with Others" pages; and lastly, for foolproof party plans, the "Party Play" games will have you covered.

Using your child's age as a starting point, and then pinpointing the play circumstances—one child or two, indoors or out, active or creative play—will help you navigate through this book and find games that are just right for your child (and his playmates) and just right for this moment of play. Enjoy the freedom to move through the pages of this book to discover games that will engage your child. And then encourage your child to tweak the games to suit his style, interests, and abilities.

If your child has a physical delay or disability, or cognitive, social, or speech delays or disabilities, you'll find hundreds of games in these pages that offer fabulous opportunities for your child to have fun and at the same time work on targeted goals, such as increasing muscle strength, cardiovascular endurance, or motor or speech development. Perhaps, for example, your child has trouble flexing his arms or reaching and grasping. There are loads of catching and tossing activities to help fine-tune those skills. Some of these games use balls of various sizes, and others use beanbags, which may make tossing, catching, and grasping a bit easier for a child with motor delays or disabilities. (You can even substitute a silk neck scarf for a ball or beanbag to invent a new variation of catch that allows extra time for catching the floating scarf.) As in all cases, you know your child best. Select games (and invent variations) that

> "The very brain circuits that are activated during play are also activated during joyous, happy moments in our lives, and the more you exercise a brain circuit, the stronger it gets. So letting kids have a good time in play is one of the healthiest things you can do for them."
>
> **—Daniel Goleman, PhD**
> psychologist and author of
> *Emotional Intelligence* and
> *Social Intelligence*

TOYS FOR CHILDREN WITH SPECIAL NEEDS

Specialized toys are available for children with motor delays or impairment, visual or hearing impairment, language delays, and a range of other special needs. Beyond Play toys is an online source to help you find toys and play suggestions tailored to your child's abilities. Their website, www.beyondplay.com, features over 1,000 toys and products you can order directly, along with useful articles and play tips. The Search by Product feature helps you find toys suited to your child's abilities and developmental stage.

allow just the right balance of challenge and success. When you discover a game that hits this mark, you'll know—your child will want to play again and again.

If your child has difficulty picking up on social cues, many of the Play with Others games are perfect to practice speaking, listening, and watching. When it comes to progress through play, the key element that seems to grease the wheel is engaging your child in a way that his interest is in high gear. And when he is interested, he is also motivated.

I am inspired time and time again by the commitment parents bring to adapting play to a child's individual needs, whether or not that child has special needs. You as a parent are first and foremost focused on your child's abilities (rather than disabilities) and you can use these abilities as the starting point for play. If you are a creative thinker, you are constantly brainstorming ways to enhance and adapt your child's play.

And believe me, a can-do, infectious attitude will get passed along to (and absorbed by) your children.

And don't think the opportunities to "seize the play" end here. One of my favorite play traditions has its own special section in this book. I'm talking about Family Game Night, a wonderful way to put your own seal of approval on the importance of play. In the Family Game Night section, you'll find different ideas for activities and games for the entire family to play together. This might mean parents and the kids, or maybe even grandparents and cousins too. There are silly games, challenging quizzes, high-energy antics, and quiet kitchen table games you can play while digging into a big tray of lasagna. You'll find everything you need to plan your very own family tradition of playtime, once a week or once a month. These special times will be remembered long after that rousing round of Beanbag Horseshoes is over.

So what are you waiting for? Go forth and seize the play!

I think favorite tried and tested games depend a little on the child. You need to watch your child carefully and see what it is that your child enjoys, because your child's an individual and not necessarily like everybody else's."

—Dorothy Einon, PhD
author of *How Children Learn Through Play*

GRADE SCHOOL PLAY

AGES 6 TO 10

Children six to ten years old are sophisticated players. They create elaborate hideouts and build impressive forts. They learn to read and write and can solve mysteries, play word games, invent outlandish tall tales, and create treasure maps. They are capable of a tremendous range of physical play (chasing, throwing, catching, dribbling, twirling, and bike riding). They can follow rules and remember directions; they can also make up their own rules as they play. All these possibilities add up to nonstop fun, but beyond all this excitement, there is a complex world of learning and growing going on. Here is a glimpse of how six-to-ten-year-olds develop through play.

PHYSICAL DEVELOPMENT Children develop and refine large muscles, coordination, strength, stamina, and balance when they run, climb, kick a ball, ride a bike, walk a plank, do somersaults and cartwheels, jump rope, and chase. They strengthen hand-eye coordination when they bounce, catch, and swat a ball, and by doing arts and crafts, along with building and construction play. Through active play, they learn to challenge themselves and set goals, they discover their interests and talents, and, last but not least, they form fitness habits that will last a lifetime.

INTELLECTUAL DEVELOPMENT As they play, grade-schoolers are expanding their minds. They sharpen their memory and practice the application of logic. They learn to brainstorm,

A WEE BIT OF HELP

In general, children six to ten are capable and competent solo players, but they still benefit from well-placed grown-up help from time to time. Try setting up any props and toys the first time a game is played so that your child sees and experiences the game as it's intended. Give a short demo to show how to use a new tool, an art material, or a building supply for creative projects. Some old classics (like Jacks or Clapping Call-Ball) may even require you to dust off your own playing skills. And when it comes to creative and imaginative activities (involving drawing or storytelling, for example), it helps to be a clever brainstorming mentor so your child becomes comfortable with the creative process of thinking up her own ideas (and so she'll see that the sky's the limit). When she asks, "What can I write?" respond with a few questions rather than an answer. If she's stumped about how to begin her story about Charlie the neighborhood cat, you might ask, "Well, what sort of hat could you imagine Charlie wearing if he decided to wear a hat? Where would he go once he had that hat on? How might he travel if he weren't walking on his own four feet?" When it comes to solo play, it's best to think of yourself as a play mentor rather than a micromanager so your child can take over and direct the play.

hypothesize, and problem solve. They discover math concepts such as patterns and sequencing. They learn about the complexities of science and nature. They expand and refine their use of language and improve their reading skills. They find ways to express their own unique thoughts and ideas through music, dance, poems, stories, drawings, paintings, and crafts.

SOCIAL AND EMOTIONAL DEVELOPMENT As children six to ten play, they learn to read facial expressions and body language. When they navigate through group play, they begin to cooperate, share, negotiate, and take turns. On a deeper level, they learn values like empathy, fairness, loyalty, and trust. They even learn from their negative play experiences, figuring out how to rebound from rejection, develop patience, manage their emotions, and control their behavior. They also make the brilliant discovery that playing is a good way to find a friend.

SAFE GRADE SCHOOL PLAY

As your child grows, she'll become increasingly involved in keeping herself safe as she plays. She will begin to understand a bit more about the dangers of traffic and strangers. For the most part, children at this age tend to like the security of having rules in place, which can be used to your advantage. While you won't be able to prevent every sprained ankle, you can work to sidestep serious injuries and danger. Here are some safety ideas to keep in mind for the six-to-ten-year-old child:

▸ Set up firm rules about where your child is and isn't allowed to play.

- Set up a rule that your child must ask for permission before he can leave your yard.
- Make your home a kid-friendly environment. (Healthy snacks are a big plus!) Provide supervision, maintain a cheerful attitude, and step in when safety issues, like violent or dangerous play, arise.
- Set up a helmet or helmet and knee pads rule for bicycling, using in-line skates, and skateboarding.
- Absolutely, positively, keep matches and lighters out of reach, and set up clear rules forbidding play with matches or fire.
- Supervise your child on swing sets, slides, and jungle gyms.
- Clearly convey safety rules and the need for supervision to all of your childcare providers or teenage babysitters.
- Check the National Program for Playground Safety website (www.playgroundsafety.org) to receive up-to-date information about backyard (residential) and public playground safety.

THE WELL-STOCKED GRADE SCHOOL TOY CUPBOARD

If you stock it, they will play! See page 253 for a list of my favorite toys and games to inspire lively, freewheeling play for six- to ten-year-olds. Also embedded in that list are all of the toys and miscellaneous household items needed for every single game or activity in this book.

CRANKY COMPANION OR SLEEP-DEPRIVED CHILD?

Did you know that children six to ten years old need nine to twelve hours of sleep each night in order to be at their best? Recent studies show that many children are not getting enough sleep, and it often shows up in their behavior with friends and family. A sleep-deprived child may get frustrated or hyperactive and have meltdowns more easily as he plays. He may be more aggressive with playmates, have trouble following rules, or lack the energy to engage in physical play. Take a quick look at how much sleep your child is getting each and every night. If your child is not getting between nine and twelve hours of sleep on a regular basis, it's time to make some changes—you might just see a big improvement in playtime behavior!

1

SOLO PLAY

What good things can happen when your six-to-ten-year-old child plays alone? He builds muscles, strength, and stamina through physical play. As he runs around outside, he burns off the nervous energy he's accumulated by sitting in school all day. He winds down from an active, busy day with quiet play. He invents and creates and figures out how things work. He watches intently and predicts what might happen next. He gets big ideas and discovers which ones work and which ones flop. He begins to see the steps it takes to turn an idea into action. And, let's not forget, he learns to entertain himself, without electronic toys and without an adult.

66

Research shows us very clearly that electronic playmates do not evoke the same brain response that being with a real human does, and that a child's future success is going to be very much determined by the way he or she is able to relate to other people and work in a group and negotiate."

—Jane M. Healy, PhD
educational psychologist and author of *Your Child's Growing Mind* and
Failure to Connect: How Computers Affect Our Children's Minds

INDOOR PLAY

Children like to be in charge of their own play. But there will be days when even the most self-directed child says, "I'm bored." Here are some ideas to jump-start traditional independent play, as well as some lively games that can be played using everyday household materials. As time goes by, these games may become like familiar old friends—comforting, go-to escapes at the end of a long school day. Perhaps your child is taken by Jacks, which challenges her to improve or refine her skills each time she plays. Or the classic paper Fortune-Teller that adds a little magic to an afternoon. Or Construction Play for problem solving. In many of these games, your role as a parent is to nudge the play at the start and let your child take it from there.

BALLOON BREEZE OBSTACLE COURSE

AGE:
6–10 years

CATEGORY:
Solo Play/
Indoor

**NUMBER OF
CHILDREN:**
One or more

A little finesse goes a long way in getting around this indoor obstacle course with a balloon bouncing on a paper plate.

Materials
▸ Large oval balloons*
▸ Large, sturdy paper plate (oval plate works best)
▸ Timer

Setup

Blow up one or two balloons. Create and mark off a simple obstacle course indoors, using chairs, cardboard boxes, and pillows as the obstacles.

Play

Your child holds the paper plate with two hands and uses it to bounce the balloon into the air continuously as he weaves around, over, and under the obstacles. To make it more challenging, set the timer for a short amount of time. As your child gets the hang of this game, he can bounce the balloon higher and higher.

2 BALLOON PUTT

Turn this game into a miniature golf–like obstacle course, using a balloon and a flyswatter to putt the balloon from place to place. Set the timer and see how many times your child can get around the course before it buzzes.

CAR AND RAMPS

3

AGE:
6–10 years

CATEGORY:
Solo Play/
Indoor

**NUMBER OF
CHILDREN:**
One or more

* SAFETY ALERT
To prevent
injury, make sure
no one stands
by the end of
the ramp.

*Here are some creative challenges to help
encourage miniature-car play.*

Materials

▶ Cardboard or foam board
▶ Hardcover books
▶ Miniature cars and trucks
▶ Shallow bowl filled with water
▶ Hula-Hoop

Jump-start

NO FLIP Using cardboard and stacked books,
your child makes a high ramp for the cars to
race down without having them flip over.*

LAUNCH He creates a ramp for the cars, then
places a shallow bowl of water near the end
of the ramp, and sees how many cars he can
"launch" into the bowl.

HULA He places a small Hula-Hoop near the
end of the ramp and sees how many cars he
can get to land inside without bouncing out.

BOUNCING BAZOOKA BULL'S-EYE

AGE:
6–10 years

CATEGORY:
Solo Play/
Indoor

NUMBER OF CHILDREN:
One or more
(a good practice
game for one,
and a competitive
game for two)

*The bouncing balls have a mind of their own,
so scoring in this game presents a real challenge!*

Materials

▸ Laundry basket

▸ Large unbreakable bowl

▸ Yardstick

▸ Ping-Pong balls, tennis balls, or small rubber balls

Setup

This game should be played against a wall clear of furniture. Position the laundry basket snugly up against the wall. Place the large bowl on the floor, 3 feet in front of the laundry basket. Use the yardstick to create a pitching line 6 to 8 feet away from the wall.

Play

Your child stands behind the pitching line and tosses the Ping-Pong ball against any area of the wall, trying to get the ball to land either inside the basket or inside the bowl for a bull's-eye. Each ball must bounce against the wall before dropping inside the basket or bowl in order to score a point. Score 5 points for each ball in the basket and 10 points for each ball in the bowl. If a ball bounces inside the bowl and bounces out again, score 7 points.

BUTTON BOWL

AGE:
6–10 years

CATEGORY:
Solo Play/
Indoor

**NUMBER OF
CHILDREN:**
One or more

* SAFETY ALERT

Due to choking
hazard, play this
game clear of
young children
or pets. Clean up
all buttons after
playing.

I bet I can do it with my eyes closed!

Materials

- 5 or more unbreakable bowls or cooking pans
- Scissors
- Black construction paper
- Invisible tape
- Sunglasses
- Plastic coffee cup with handle
- Assorted buttons
- Timer

Setup

Mark a pitching line across the floor. Position the bowls in a vertical line in incremental distances from the pitching line, starting about 4 feet away. Assign each of these bowls a score, starting with one point for the closest bowl, two points for the next, and so on. Next, make a simple "blindfold" by cutting two ovals from the construction paper and taping them to the lenses of the sunglasses. Fill the plastic cup with buttons.

Play*

Your child sets the timer for one to two minutes and gets in position behind the pitching line. She grabs the button cup with one hand and puts the blindfold glasses on. Then she pitches the buttons toward the bowls until the timer goes off. When the buzzer sounds, she'll add up all the points scored by figuring out how many buttons landed in each bowl and doing some simple math.

6 **BUTTON BOWL SCATTER**

For an easier version of this game, omit the blindfold and simply scatter pie pans or cake pans across the floor at varying distances from the pitching line. Assign points to each pie pan.

7 **LIBRARY NIGHT**

PARENT
TIP

"Reading is very important in our household. To eliminate boredom with books that have already been read, we've come up with 'Library Night.' Once a month, we bring out the children's books we've picked up in the weeks prior at yard sales and thrift stores. We set up a 'library' on the kitchen table and distribute handmade library cards (index cards) to our kids so they can 'check out' a couple of books. Then we put the latest collection in a cardboard box with the spines facing out and let the children select books. When they've grown tired of these books, we donate them back to our local thrift store and search for more used books for next month."

—Colleen from Indiana

8 | JACKS

AGE:
6–10 years

CATEGORY:
Solo Play/
Indoor

**NUMBER OF
CHILDREN:**
One or more

* SAFETY ALERT
Due to choking
hazard, play this
game clear of
young children
or pets. Clean
up all jacks after
playing.

*A first-rate traditional game that works well as
practice play for one player.*

CLASSIC
ACTIVITY

Materials

▶ Set of plastic or metal jacks
▶ Small rubber ball

Setup

Find a smooth floor on which to play.

Play

There are five traditional ways to play the
game of jacks, each with its own distinct level
of difficulty. Each version of the game begins
with the player tossing the jacks onto the floor
so that they scatter in one small area.

9 BASIC JACKS

With one hand, the player tosses the ball into
the air, picks up one jack, and catches the ball
after one bounce. Tossing the ball again, he
picks up one more jack (keeping the first jack
in his hand) and catches the ball after one
bounce. He continues picking up one jack at a
time in this way until all the jacks have been
collected in his hand.

10 ONESIES, TWOSIES, THREESIES

After the first round, the player scatters the
jacks on the floor again, and this time picks up
two jacks at a time, still catching the ball after
one bounce. He scatters the jacks again and

picks up three at a time. The player continues by picking up four at a time, five at a time, and so on until the final round of play when he scoops up all ten jacks at one time. (If the player falls short of his goal, he tries to scoop up the remaining jacks in one try.)

11 EGGS IN THE BASKET

Player tosses the ball, picks up one jack (or more) at a time, and quickly moves the jack(s) to his free hand before catching the ball.

12 CRACK THE EGGS

This version adds one extra step to Eggs in the Basket. The player must tap each jack on the ground with the scooping hand (pretending to crack an egg) before moving the jack(s) to the free hand.

13 DOUBLE BOUNCE

To ease up the challenge a bit, the player takes on any of the jack variations, allowing the ball to bounce twice before catching it.

14 JACKS FOR TWO

Any of the traditional jacks games above can be played with two or more players. In this scenario, one player starts the game and continues to take turns tossing the ball and scooping up jacks as long as he catches the ball on one bounce and scoops up the predetermined number of jacks. When he doesn't catch the ball on one bounce or grab the correct number of jacks, his turn is over and the second player takes a turn.

PAPER AIRPLANE

AGE:
6–10 years

CATEGORY:
Solo Play/
Indoor

**NUMBER OF
CHILDREN:**
One or more

*Every child should know how to make old-
fashioned paper airplanes. Here's a basic
design to get you started.*

Materials

▶ Copy or computer paper (8½ inches by 11 inches)

Create

1. Fold the paper in half lengthwise, make a
crease, and unfold it.

2. Holding the paper vertically, fold each top
corner into the center crease, creating two
equal-size triangle flaps.

3. Fold the right diagonal edge of the plane in
to line up with the center crease. Then fold
the left diagonal edge in to line up with the
same center crease.

4. Flip the plane over and fold the new right
diagonal edge in to line up with the center
crease. Then fold the new left diagonal edge
in to line up with the center crease. This
creates a sturdy nose for your plane.

5. Flip the plane over, and fold the left edge of
the plane over to meet the right (using the
original crease from step 1).

6. There should be three layers of folds on the left side. Pinch the middle fold between your thumb and index finger to create the fuselage of the plane. The other two folds become the wings. Let 'er fly!

16 FLYING HIGH

To create a slightly different plane (and different flying capabilities), vary the width of the crease in step 4 above, so that the fuselage—where you hold the plane—is narrow, medium, or extremely wide.

FORTUNE-TELLER

AGE:
6–10 years

CATEGORY:
Solo Play/
Indoor

**NUMBER OF
CHILDREN:**
One or more

What fortune and fun does that piece of paper hold in its magical folds? Children today still find these fun to make and entertaining to play with.

Materials

▸ Copy or computer paper

▸ Pen

▸ Scissors

Create

1. Cut an 8½-by-8½-inch square from a sheet of paper and lay it flat on the table.

2. Fold one corner to the opposite corner, making a diagonal crease. Open the paper, and fold it diagonally in the other direction. Make a crease, and open the paper.

3. Fold each of the four corners into the center.

4. Flip the paper over, and fold the new corners into the center.

5. Write a number from one to eight in each of the small triangles on this side of the paper.

6. Open each of the numbered flaps and write eight different messages inside. Close the flaps.

7. Flip the folded paper over and write the name of a different color on each of the four squares.

8. Fold the fortune-teller in half so that the four colors are facing out.

9. Position the thumb and index finger of each hand underneath the flaps, finessing the folds a bit so that the fingers are in each of the four points.

Play

Your child holds his fortune-teller with the color flaps showing. He asks his friend to pick a color. If the color is blue, your child flaps his fingers back and forth one time for each letter in the word: *b-l-u-e* (four times). Then he asks his friend to select one of the numbers on the four flaps that are showing. He moves his fingers back and forth as he counts out the number. At last, his friend selects one of the numbers showing, and that flap is lifted to reveal the fortune.

CONSTRUCTION PLAY

AGE:
6–10 years

CATEGORY:
Solo Play/
Indoor

**NUMBER OF
CHILDREN:**
One or more

*The six-to-ten-year-old crowd are sophisticated
thinkers and problem solvers, ready for hours of
open-ended construction toy play.*

Materials

▶ LEGOs (or other interlocking building blocks)

Jump-start

LEGOs can be turned into airplanes, cars,
tanks, rockets, robots, monsters, houses, and
much more. How many different vehicles can
your child make? Have your child build a
replica of your house (and neighboring homes),
garage, deck. How many buildings can your
child make in 20 minutes?

19 TINKERTOYS*

These plastic wheels, spokes, and connectors
come with a design guide to help children
get ideas on how to get started and what to
make. Follow the directions in the box to
create amazing structures. Use your own
imagination to invent another way of building
each of these structures. Build a crazy
"contraption." Challenge your child to build
another one exactly like it. Create prehistoric
creatures or extraterrestrial beings.

KITCHEN TABLE PLAY

Although children six to ten years old are much more independent than preschoolers, they still enjoy the comfort of playing alongside a parent. With these solo play kitchen activities, I've also included some terrific thinking and guessing games that your child can either play alone (with pencil and paper to jot down guesses) or with you, as you prepare dinner nearby.

20 COMIC STRIP

AGE:
6–10 years

CATEGORY:
Solo Play/
Indoor

**NUMBER OF
CHILDREN:**
One or more

Who says that comics have to be saved for Sundays?

Materials

▶ Artist sketchbook

▶ Pencil and kneaded eraser

▶ Assorted fine-tipped color markers

Jump-start

Challenge your child to create her own comic strip. The characters she invents might be from her own life or far-out fantasy creatures with their own language. Have her write a few notes to herself to create a life for her main character (how old are they, where do they live, who are their friends, what is their special talent, what do they like to eat). Sketching out a drawing will help capture the character's extraordinary features. Have that drawing lead to the action and conversations that follow, frame by frame.

TEN-IN-SIXTY

AGE:
6–10 years

CATEGORY:
Solo Play/
Indoor

**NUMBER OF
CHILDREN:**
One or more

Guess ten names in sixty seconds in this quick-moving game.

Materials

▶ Scissors

▶ Paper

▶ Pencil

▶ Unbreakable bowl

▶ Baby name book

▶ Timer

Setup

Your child selects any 20 letters from the alphabet. She cuts 20 small pieces of paper, and writes one of these letters on each piece; she then folds the pieces of paper in half, places them in a bowl, and mixes them around. She can skim through the baby name book to familiarize herself with names (and spellings) that begin with each of those 20 letters before the guessing begins.

Play

Your child sets the timer for 60 seconds (or longer if needed). She draws a letter from the bowl and, without consulting the names book, quickly begins writing down names starting with this letter, with the goal of writing down at least 10 names before the buzzer sounds. When the buzzer sounds, she scores herself one point for each name on the list. She continues drawing letters from the bowl, setting the timer, and writing down as many names as possible. She can set a goal of jotting down 100 or 200 total names before dinnertime. (To increase the challenge, she can then use the baby name book to check the spelling of each name on her list. Points are scored only for those names spelled correctly in this version of the game.)

22 TEN-IN-THIRTY

This version of the game is played by one child and one grown-up, and typically less time is needed, since you are not writing down each name but calling it out. The child selects a letter from the bowl and you call out as many names as possible (before the buzzer sounds) that begin with the selected letter. During the next round of play, the child selects a letter for herself, and she must call out at least 10 names before the buzzer sounds. Play for fun, or if you prefer, keep score, with one point scored for each name.

> Chess has very simple rules. Any adult can learn in under an hour with no problem. One famous book is *Bobby Fischer Teaches Chess*. That's a classic. It will guide a parent into learning how to play the game, and from there they'll have some competence in how to teach their children to play."
>
> **—Maurice Ashley**
> international chess grand master and author of
> *Chess for Success: Using an Old Game to
> Build New Strengths in Children and Teens*

PUZZLER MIX-UP

AGE:
6–10 years

CATEGORY:
Solo Play/
Indoor

**NUMBER OF
CHILDREN:**
One

Making the puzzles is part of the fun, but scrambling through the pieces to put three puzzles together simultaneously adds challenge!

Materials

▸ 3 interesting full-page color photos from a magazine

▸ Nontoxic white glue

▸ Poster board

▸ Scissors

▸ Large plastic bag

▸ Timer

Setup

Your child selects three full-page color photos from a magazine. (Photos with distinct colors featuring children, animals, or objects of interest are best.) He glues each of the three photos to a piece of cardboard or poster board, then cuts each photo into 12 or more puzzle pieces. The pieces of all three puzzles are tossed into the bag and shaken up.

Play

Your child sets the timer for 5 to 8 minutes (adjusting the time as needed to create just the right challenge). With all the jumbled puzzle pieces spread out on the kitchen table, he begins piecing together all three puzzles, trying to complete the task before the buzzer sounds. (If he wishes to keep score, he can count out the number of loose puzzle pieces left on the table after the buzzer has sounded, scoring one point for each remaining piece on the table, with "0" being the top score.)

24 BLIND SKETCHING

AGE:
6–10 years

CATEGORY:
Solo Play/
Indoor

NUMBER OF CHILDREN:
One or more

No peeking at the drawings. There'll be lots of guesses from the peanut gallery when they're done.

Materials

▸ Pencils, markers, or crayons

▸ Newsprint or drawing paper

▸ Bandana

Setup

Your child makes a list of 10 things that she is able to draw with some measure of accuracy (a building, tree, pet, hand, face, leaf, flower, bicycle, frying pan, or coffee cup, for example).

Play

After placing some pieces of newsprint paper on the table in front of her, your child ties the bandana around her head, blindfolding herself so that she cannot see the paper. On each piece of paper, she draws a picture of one of the items on her list, developing her collection of mystery drawings. She then holds up each drawing to see if any family member can guess what the items are supposed to be. (She gets to choose to reveal her list of items or not.)

ALPHABET GARDEN

AGE:
6–10 years

CATEGORY:
Solo Play/
Indoor

**NUMBER OF
CHILDREN:**
One

*A is for apples, B is for beans. There's an alphabet
in your garden that's ripe for the picking.*

Materials

▸ Garden seed catalog

▸ Large sheet of poster board

▸ Pencils or markers

Setup

To create the Alphabet Garden chart, your child
prints one letter of the alphabet (from *A* to *Z*)
along the left edge of the poster board, placing
only one letter per line.

Play

Paging through the catalog, your child finds
vegetables and herbs that start with every
letter of the alphabet; when he finds a plant,

GROWING VEGGIES

Kids get a big kick out of harvesting their own veggies. If your
family lives in a city, you can still plant on a windowsill. The
following are well suited to container gardening: tomatoes, leaf
lettuce, peppers, eggplant, squash, green onions, green beans,
radishes, parsley, and cucumbers. Check seed catalogs for
varieties best suited to your climate and growing conditions.

he writes its name on the appropriate letter line. (He might need help with some of the more difficult words.) At the end of the game, tally up the total foods for every letter.

26 DRAW ME A STORY

AGE:
6–10 years

CATEGORY:
Solo Play/
Indoor

NUMBER OF CHILDREN:
One or more

Sometimes the pictures come first when bringing a story to life.

Materials

▸ Artist sketchbook or journal
▸ Pencil and kneaded eraser
▸ Assorted fine-tipped color markers

Jump-start

Most children respond to the idea of creating one main character (such as a fantasy creature, futuristic insect, person, or animal) to start their story. From this simple beginning, your child can go on to imagine what the character looks like, what they wear, where they live, who their friends are, and what exciting event has just happened in their life. From these drawings and sketches and jotted-down details, a story tends to follow. If he doesn't like what he's drawn or written, he can use the eraser freely or add and delete pages using scissors and tape.

DOG DIARIES

AGE:
6–10 years

CATEGORY:
Solo Play/
Indoor

NUMBER OF CHILDREN:
One or more

Write a story about what you think the little brown dog next door does when he thinks no one is watching.

Materials

▸ Notebook or small journal

▸ Pencils

▸ Colored pencils or markers

▸ Photos (optional)

Setup

Ask your child to imagine what a particular neighborhood dog (or family dog) might do if traveling about the neighborhood freely. Brainstorm about favorite discoveries in the neighborhood, foods, games to play, and other animal friends.

Play

Your child starts the Dog Diaries by writing down the names of all the dogs in the neighborhood, or by inventing a group of imaginary dogs of various shapes and sizes. Next, she writes a short description of each dog. They might have distinctive or funny haircuts, hats, and accessories. After the characters have been created, pick one or two dogs and write about their imaginary adventures for the day. Where did they travel? What did they see? What treats did they find to eat? What kind

of mischief did they get into? If you and your child sit down once a week to create a new chapter, this diary can keep going for quite some time.

28 CAT CHRONICLES

No need to offend the cat lovers in the group! Kids can create lively tales with their favorite felines as the main characters as well.

> Be sure not to overschedule and overcontrol and overmanage all your child's free time, because those down moments, when kids just get together on their own and do what they want, are the most joyous. Some parents get into being overachievers and wanting their child to master the violin and be the best soccer player and also learn ballet. That's well and good, but you want to be sure not to squelch all the time for play."
>
> **—Daniel Goleman, PhD**
> psychologist and author of
> *Emotional Intelligence* and *Social Intelligence*

TALL TALES

AGE:
6–10 years

CATEGORY:
Solo Play/
Indoor

**NUMBER OF
CHILDREN:**
One or more

*Turn writing and brainstorming into a fun game
that makes it easy to come up with story ideas.*

Materials

▸ Paper

▸ Scissors

▸ Pencil

▸ 2 large yogurt or cottage cheese
containers with lids

Setup

Cut 20 small pieces of paper. Select 10 letters
of the alphabet that can be readily associated
with names; write each letter on a piece of
paper. Fold these papers in half and toss them
into one of the plastic containers, stirring them
around. Think of 10 animals or creatures (real
or imaginary) and write the name of each on a
piece of paper. Fold these papers in half, toss
them in the second plastic container, and mix
them around.

Play

The child selects a slip of paper from each
container. He invents a name for the animal,
starting with the chosen letter, and writes an
action-packed, silly, or unbelievable story
about what his character did or discovered
today. Some children may need idea starters—
What happened with Martha the Goat on

the playground today? Where did she go on vacation? What happened when she went to the grocery store? Older children can write the stories down on paper and read them to the family at dinner. Younger children may wish to tell their story as they invent it.

66

When parents decide to limit their child's video games and screen time, yeah, the kids will scream, and then the next thing you know, they'll be outside playing. It happens at my house all the time. The 'Oh, woe is me' lasts a minute or two, and then the next thing you know, they're engaged in something much better for them. So I'm willing to take that heat."

—Edward Hallowell, MD
psychiatrist and author of
Driven to Distraction and *CrazyBusy*

RHYMIN' SIMON

AGE:
6–10 years

CATEGORY:
Solo Play/
Indoor

**NUMBER OF
CHILDREN:**
One or more

*There may be a future songwriter or poet in your
midst. All she needs is a little nudge to get the
talent flowing.*

Materials

▸ A book with classic poems and counting rhymes

▸ Journal (or paper)

▸ Pencils

Setup

Select one classic poem or counting rhyme to
use as a template.

Play

Your child keeps the first line of the rhyme,
but continues the game by adding her own
original rhymes thereafter to invent a new
poem with new characters and action. To get
started, here are the first lines from several
nursery rhymes:

Hickory, dickory, dock

Baa, baa, black sheep, have you any wool?

Two little blackbirds sitting on a hill

Higglety pigglety pop!

One, two, three, . . . (*add your own next line*)
Four, five, six, . . . (*add another line*)

ARTS & CRAFTS

Children love to draw and paint and create. Behind the scenes, life skills are being developed in subtle ways. Your child learns to improvise, problem solve, and tolerate frustration when things go awry. She also sees that sometimes a mistake is a new beginning, and the end product is something more spectacular than originally planned. She learns patience and perseverance. She may also discover that she can escape the busy pace of life when she paints, draws, or creates, and this is a lesson to carry forward for many years to come. Here are some open-ended art ideas with room for individual creativity and experimentation.

31 DRAWING

AGE:
6–10 years

CATEGORY:
Solo Play/
Indoor

**NUMBER OF
CHILDREN:**
One or more

Call it doodling, sketching, or designing; every child needs paper to draw on.

Materials

▸ 24 felt-tip fine-point color markers (available at art supply stores)

▸ Multipurpose paper (for practice drawing)

▸ Drawing paper or sketch pad

▸ Cardboard blotter

Create

All you really need to get started is paper and markers or pencils and a good, flat, hard surface for drawing, like the kitchen table. Some children will be satisfied making abstract designs with shapes and colors that spontaneously come to life. Others will ask, "What should I draw?" and will need a bit of brainstorming help to settle on an object or a person of interest to represent through their drawing. Some like to chat or listen to music while they doodle or draw. Others become engrossed in an imaginative process that is surrounded by silence.

32 PENCIL DRAWING

Children six to ten will appreciate the wide assortment of real artist's pencils that are available at art supply stores. Every artist could also use a real artist's eraser: a kneaded eraser that erases without leaving behind any pink traces.

33 CHALK PASTELS

For a different drawing experience, use colored chalk with colored construction paper, sketch paper, poster board, or mat board, which has a rough texture that can create distinctive drawings.

ART SUPPLIES

A well-stocked art supply store should have a complete line of art supplies just right for children. I am always amazed at what I can find to keep children busy creating, without breaking the bank. Here are a few of the things you might find there:

- Acrylic paints
- Art bins and tackle boxes
- Artist's easel
- Artist's portfolio
- Beads and string
- Blank journals
- Cardboard boxes
- Chalk
- Chenille craft stems (aka pipe cleaners)
- Child-safe scissors
- Colored pencils
- Craft dough cutters
- Craft sticks (aka Popsicle sticks)
- Crayons
- Crepe paper or streamers
- Drawing boards
- Drawing pencils
- Eyedroppers
- Face paint
- Fine-tip pens (assorted colors in a set)
- Finger paints
- Giant foam board (40 inches by 60 inches)
- Glitter (and glitter glue)
- Ink pad and stamps
- Modeling clay
- Nontoxic glue
- Oil pastels (crayons)
- Paintbrushes and rollers
- Paper of every size and texture
- Play dough
- Poster board
- Precut mat boards (to frame drawings)
- Printing supplies (sponges, paints, and paper)
- Rolls of butcher paper
- Single-hole punch
- Spill-proof paint containers
- Tempera paints
- Washable paints (nontoxic)

NOTE: If your local store has mainly adult supplies, children's art supplies can also be purchased from online art supplies vendors such as www.artistcraftsman.com.

DESIGN A CASTLE

AGE:
6–10 years

CATEGORY:
Solo Play/
Indoor

**NUMBER OF
CHILDREN:**
One or more

*The sky is the limit to all the brainstorming that
can take place when your child designs his castle.*

Materials

▸ Drawing paper

▸ Pencil

▸ Kneaded eraser

Jump-start

If you asked your child to draw a realistic
picture of the outside of a castle, with all its
turrets and steeples, he might be stumped.
But if you ask him to design the inside of a
thirty-room castle, now that's another matter.
The interior rooms can be drawn as squares
and rectangles, with bold lines to show the
placement of doors and windows. Secret
passageways, leading to underground rooms
that no one knows about, can be added. On
separate sheets of paper, elaborate inventions
can be designed for cooking and cleanup in
the kitchen. Ingenious communication devices
might be invented and illustrated, to alert the
lord and lady when an intruder arrives. In fact,
he may save all these floor plan designs and
pages of inventions in a Design Notebook and
add to it when a new idea strikes.

Once your child has tackled the castle
design, see the variations on the next page for
some other design challenges to try.

35 SPACE STATION

Design the interior of a spaceship, rocket, time-travel machine, or futuristic car.

36 THE HIGH SEAS

Design the inside of a pirate ship, a sailboat that travels around the world, or a futuristic submarine.

37 ANIMAL HOUSE

Design a barn or zoo that would have inventions all sorts of animals might request if they could talk.

38 PLAN FOR THE FUTURE

Create the floor plans of houses you might live in 10 years, 20 years, and then 50 years from now.

66

Every human being has the capacity to create—not only the capacity, but the need to create. To create is part of inner growth."

—Michele Cassou
artist and author of *Kids Play: Igniting Children's Creativity* and *Life, Paint and Passion: Reclaiming the Magic of Spontaneous Expression*

ONE GIANT FLOOR DRAWING

AGE:
6–10 years

CATEGORY:
Solo Play/
Indoor

NUMBER OF CHILDREN:
One or more

Here's a BIG idea that is sure to get your child's attention!

Materials

▶ Roll of butcher paper

▶ Invisible tape

▶ Crayons or washable markers

Setup

Cover the entire kitchen floor (or one large area of the floor) with long strips of butcher paper on a day when foot traffic in the kitchen can be restricted for a few hours. Use invisible tape to adhere the paper to the floor and tape the seams together so you have one giant, super-duper sheet of drawing paper. (Set up some rules about keeping crayon marks off the cupboards, baseboards, and floor, and decide in advance if this drawing will be saved afterward or sent to the recycling bin.)

Create

Give your child a pack of crayons or washable markers and let her have the pleasure of making a huge drawing of her own choosing. Some children may decide to make one continuous drawing or design, others may create a make-believe village with roads for toy cars, and others may write stories, songs, or poems. This is a fun way to give your child's creativity a big space to blossom, and it might also appeal to a child who has previously been reluctant to draw or make art.

HONOR YOUR CHILD'S ARTWORK

▶ Designate one large frame (with glass and wire for hanging) for each child in the family. When your child creates a new drawing, pastel, or painting, slip it inside the frame and hang it on the wall. Continue to rotate your child's latest paintings into the frame as new work is created.

▶ Use both sides of your child's bedroom door as "art gallery space" on which to hang drawings and paintings.

▶ Tape a featured artwork of the week to the inside of your front door.

▶ Have a few of your child's special paintings or drawings matted and hung permanently at home.

▶ Save your child's artwork in a safe place and have a family art show once or twice a year. Display all of the artwork in one or two rooms of your home. Have a little family party to celebrate the "opening."

▶ Send artwork to relatives and friends who live far away.

▶ Create greeting cards and note cards from your child's drawings.

40 | PAINTING

AGE:
6–10 years

CATEGORY:
Solo Play/
Indoor

NUMBER OF CHILDREN:
One or more

There's no rule that says painting is always about representing real objects. Sometimes painting is all about color, shapes, and imagination.

Materials

- Vinyl tablecloth or newspapers
- Washable paints
- Assorted paintbrushes
- Several plastic containers
- Paper
- Disposable foil muffin tin or paper plate
- Recycled dress shirt (artist's smock)

Setup

Put a vinyl tablecloth or newspapers on the kitchen table to protect against spills and leaks, and assemble all your paints, brushes, water containers, and paper. Put a dab of each color in separate sections of the disposable muffin tin or spread out on the paper plate.

Create

41 PAINT STORY

Have your child illustrate a character or events in a favorite book, story, or fairy tale.

42 MY HERO

Have your child paint a fantasy character or an action hero of her own invention.

43 PAINT-A-DAY

Have her paint a picture of something funny that happened this week.

ART PORTFOLIOS

My family has a collection of my grandmother's pastel drawings and oil paintings dating back to 1915, when she was sixteen years old. She's no longer with us, but we still get pleasure from the paintings she created so many years ago. We also have my mother's artwork and many of the pen-and-ink drawings, paintings, and sculptures that I created. So when my children were young, I knew that it was important to me to find a safe place to store their creations. I purchased large professional artist's portfolios, one for each child. Storing your child's artwork may be low on your to-do list right now, but trust me, you'll thank me later. An artist's portfolio is always a good choice, but you can also use a large recycled suitcase or a plastic storage container on wheels.

44 WINDOW MIXER

Have her pick three colors (and mix them to create more colors) and paint something she sees out the window.

45 PAINT TIME TRAVEL

Have her paint a picture of what she looks like now or of what she looked like when she was a baby or a toddler.

46 SIX-FOUR

Encourage your child to make a design that fills the entire paper, using six colors and four different shapes.

FINGERPRINT COLLAGE

47

AGE:
6–10 years

CATEGORY:
Solo Play/
Indoor

**NUMBER OF
CHILDREN:**
One or more

*Who says you need paintbrushes to paint?
Getting your hands dirty is part of the fun.*

Materials

▸ Washable paints

▸ Disposable plate (plastic or hefty paper)

▸ Construction paper (or heavy, textured paper)

▸ Paper towels and water for cleanup

▸ Fine-tipped markers (optional)

▸ Sponge

Create

The artist squirts a small amount of each color in different sections of the plate. She dips a finger in one color at a time, pressing it onto the paper to create a multicolor collage of fingerprints. The prints can be clustered into shapes or spread out at random.

48 FINGERPRINT GREETING

The artist uses her pinky to create borders or designs on colored paper. She can cluster her fingerprints in the shape of flowers, wreaths, packages, and bows. The designs can then be fine-tuned or embellished using fine-tipped markers.

49 SPONGE PRINT COLLAGE

The artist cuts small squares from a sponge and dips these squares in washable paint to create a collage. (The sponges should be slightly dampened with water beforehand.) The artist can make random designs using overlaid colors, or draw an object like a tree and make it come alive by pressing dabs of colors on top. To avoid dripping, let the design dry thoroughly before moving or hanging the paper.

FISHING TACKLE ART BOX

Every creative child needs to store and organize her art supplies in one handy place. The fishing tackle art box is a perfect container for storing brushes, pencils, erasers, scissors, a hole punch, paints, bags of beads, and rolls of string. Whether you recycle a real fishing tackle box or purchase a plastic art box with compartments, you've got a good start on keeping all your child's art supplies in one place. For larger art supplies like tablets of paper, boxes of felt-tip markers and crayons, and bottles of glue, a large plastic storage tub is a good choice. (If space is limited in your home, purchase a large plastic storage container with wheels that can slide under your child's bed.) Organizing your child's art and craft supplies will enable her to easily initiate art projects on her own and also sends a clear message that being creative and making art is something that is valued and honored.

50 GLITTER-GLUE PRINTS

AGE:
6–10 years

CATEGORY:
Solo Play/
Indoor

**NUMBER OF
CHILDREN:**
One or more

* **SAFETY ALERT**
Keep glitter
and glue clear
of younger
brothers or
sisters.

Create sponge shapes (or letters), dip the sponge in glue, make an imprint on paper, and sprinkle glitter on top to make a sparkling design.

Materials

▸ Newspaper

▸ Felt-tipped marker

▸ Sponge 'Ums (compressed sheets of sponge material available at art supply stores)

▸ Scissors

▸ Nontoxic white glue*

▸ Disposable plastic plates or pie plates

▸ Several different colors of glitter*

▸ Poster board or construction paper

▸ Bowl of water

Setup

Spread the newspaper all over the table or floor before beginning this project to help contain the mess. Your child uses the felt-tipped marker to draw a shape or letter of the alphabet on a small section of a Sponge 'Um sheet, and then cuts out the shape with scissors. She continues drawing shapes and letters on the Sponge 'Ums and cutting them out so that she creates a collection of sponge shapes. Next, she pours a small amount of white glue into the plastic plate and arranges the glitter and poster board or paper on the table.

Create

First, your child should wet each sponge with water and wring out the excess. Next, she dips a sponge in the glue and places it on the poster board, pressing lightly for a few seconds to make an imprint. (The sponges should be placed on another plastic plate when not in use.) After the glue is in place, she selects one color of glitter and shakes it over the imprint. To remove the excess glitter, she tips the poster board on its side. This process is repeated with other sponges and glitter colors to create an interesting mix of shapes, colors, and textures.

51 FRONT DOOR ARTWORK

"Our front door is a giant venue for seasonal decorations, and our six-year-old just happens to love making them. We keep construction paper, scissors, and tape on hand at all times, so that whatever the season, his little hands are busy, and our front door is never bare. Two little tips: Keep a vacuum cleaner handy and be sure to have plenty of extra tape so that whatever you put on the door will stay up!"

—Ella from Virginia

52 | HOMEMADE GREETING CARDS

AGE:
6–10 years

CATEGORY:
Solo Play/
Indoor

**NUMBER OF
CHILDREN:**
One or more

*A homemade greeting card expresses so much
more than the message it contains.*

Materials

- Construction paper
- Nontoxic white glue
- Glitter
- Markers, crayons,
  colored pencils

- Scraps of brightly
  colored fabric, yarn,
  and ribbon
- Scissors
- Envelopes

Create

Your child folds each sheet of paper in half
(widthwise) or quarters to make a large or
medium-size greeting card and decorates each
card with a unique design. Fabric or paper
cutouts and shapes can be glued to the front.

53 | POP-UP GREETING CARDS

AGE:
6–10 years

CATEGORY:
Solo Play/
Indoor

**NUMBER OF
CHILDREN:**
One or more

*This three-dimensional pop-up card looks pretty
wiggly and animated, and kids love the element
of surprise.*

Materials

- Construction paper
- Scissors
- Colored pencils,
  markers, or crayons

- Glitter
- Nontoxic white glue
- Clear tape
- Envelopes

Create

Your child folds a piece of construction paper in half or quarters to make a greeting card (see activity 52), using colored pencils, markers, or crayons to decorate the front of the card. She decides what she wants the "pop-up" shape to be and outlines it in pencil on another sheet of construction paper. (Ideas might include a heart, a birthday cake, a present, the words "I Love You" or "Celebrate," etc.) She cuts out the image, following her outline, then cuts four ½-by-5-inch construction paper strips. Next, she folds each strip accordion-style (folding the end of a strip over ½ inch, then under ½ inch, over and under, to create a series of folds). To support the pop-up shape, she attaches one end of each accordion strip to the back of the pop-up shape with small pieces of clear tape; the other end of each accordion strip is taped to the inside of the card.

She can test out the mechanism by pressing the pop-up image down to make sure it pops up when released. (The length of the paper strips may need to be adjusted, depending on the size of the pop-up shape. If the strips are too long, the pop-up shape may droop; too short, and it may not "pop" enough.)

54

TATTERED AND TORN MOSAIC

AGE:
6–10 years

CATEGORY:
Solo Play/
Indoor

**NUMBER OF
CHILDREN:**
One or more

*Tear a picture or some colored construction
paper to bits and put it together to create
something entirely new.*

Materials

▸ Nontoxic white glue

▸ Small plastic yogurt container
  or margarine tub

▸ Construction paper

▸ Colored pencil

▸ Small paintbrush

Setup

The mosaic artist pours a small amount of
glue in the plastic container and adds a few
drops of water to thin the glue slightly.

Create

Your child tears construction paper into
small, random shapes, then arranges the
pieces into piles by color. He then sketches
a simple object, shape, or design on a sheet
of construction paper in colored pencil.
Working piecemeal, he paints a little glue
onto one area at a time, filling it in by sticking
on small pieces of paper to create the mosaic.

55 TATTERED AND TORN YARN

Your child makes a pencil outline on the paper. He squeezes a trail of glue all over the outline and covers it with a piece of yarn; now he fills it in with the pieces of paper to make a spiced-up paper mosaic design.

56 TATTERED AND TORN MAGAZINE MOSAIC

First, your child flips through magazines, looking for photos in vibrant colors, tearing out the photos, and arranging them in small piles according to color. Second, after writing a silly message or drawing a design on a piece of construction paper, he glues on the photo scraps to create a shiny mosaic.

57 FLOWER PETAL SPIRAL

AGE:
6–10 years

CATEGORY:
Solo Play/
Indoor

**NUMBER OF
CHILDREN:**
One

Quite an impressive collage comes to life from recycled magazines.

Materials

▸ Pencil

▸ Construction paper in various colors

▸ Scissors

▸ Flower and shrub (or garden seed) catalogs with lots of photos of colorful flower blossoms

▸ Nontoxic white glue

Setup

Using a pencil, help your child draw the spiral template to begin this design. Draw a circle about the size of a quarter in the center of the construction paper, spiraling out to create a snail-like circular design until you've filled up nearly the entire page. Don't worry about drawing perfect circles; you can use a pretty free-form oval shape.

Create

Your child cuts small pieces of flower photos from the catalogs and arranges them in color-coded piles on the table. (Lots of photos in lots of different colors are needed to fill this design.) Your child begins cutting pieces to fit the spiral and gluing them to the page in whatever design strikes her fancy. Some children may want a random, colorful design; others will use all the white flowers in a cluster in the center, for example, then cut various small pink squares to create the next progression of color. There is absolutely no wrong way to do this flower spiral.

58 PAPER MOSAIC SPIRAL

Beginning with the same snail-like pencil drawing, your child cuts small squares from various colors of construction paper and uses them to fill in the spiral. Arrange the colors in a recurring pattern or leave it to fate.

OUTDOOR PLAY

t's crucial to get your child outside during these years. As she gets older, homework, time spent at school, trips to the movies, and other indoor activities will increasingly pull at her time. The outdoors is where she gets to experience the joy of movement and soak up all those great smells, sights, and sounds that will nurture her body and her imagination for years to come. Being comfortable doing stuff outdoors is a marvelous gift to carry into adulthood. Think sports, camping, hiking, exploring, or even fixing things or painting on a sunny day—these are the experiences that outdoor play leads to.

LET'S PLAY BALL!

Here are some captivating outdoor ball games and drills for one. These games help develop tossing, dribbling, and kicking skills, strengthen hand-eye coordination, speed, and agility, and foster perseverance along the way! What's more, these active outdoor play ideas may inspire opportunities for reflective daydreaming too. As your child plays in the yard, she may be imagining walking up to bat in a Major League Baseball game or kicking the game-winning goal in a soccer championship. (As an added bonus, all of these ball games can be easily adapted for two or more players.)

SEVEN UP

AGE:
6–10 years

CATEGORY:
Solo Play/
Outdoor

**NUMBER OF
CHILDREN:**
One or more

Soft drinks not included!

Materials

▸ Sidewalk chalk

▸ Tennis ball or small rubber ball

Setup

The player will need a windowless outside wall (a garage door tends to be a good choice) against which to bounce the ball. He uses the chalk to draw a line on the pavement 5 feet or more away from the building.

Play

This game has a predetermined series of different actions the player performs while bouncing and catching the ball, starting with "onesies" and ending with "sevensies." Here are the motions for each of the seven rounds of play:

ONESIES Bounce the ball against the wall one time and catch it.

TWOSIES Bounce the ball hard on the pavement so it flies high in the air, twirl around once, and catch the ball. Repeat this action a second time.

THREESIES Bounce the ball against the wall, clap once, and catch it before it bounces. Bounce it again, clapping twice, and catch it before the bounce. Bounce the ball one more time, clap three times quickly, and catch it before it bounces.

FOURSIES Bounce the ball against the wall, clap once in front of your face, then quickly clap once behind your head, and catch the ball. Repeat this action four times.

FIVESIES Bounce the ball against the wall, slap your hands on your thighs, cross your hands over your chest, clap once, and catch the ball. Repeat this action five times.

SIXIES Throw the ball into the air, lift up your right knee and wrap your arms around it so you can clap with your arms underneath your leg, lift your left knee up and clap with your arms underneath it, and catch the ball. Repeat this three times (you should have clapped six times in total).

SEVENSIES Throw the ball up in the air under one leg and catch it. Repeat this seven times.

SOCCER DRIBBLE AND SCORE

AGE:
6–10 years

CATEGORY:
Solo Play/
Outdoor

**NUMBER OF
CHILDREN:**
One or more

Dribble, turn, tap, kick—quick, quick, quick!

Materials

▸ 4 plastic sports cones (or 4 shoes) to use as obstacles

▸ Backyard soccer net (or 2 shoes positioned approximately 8 to 10 feet apart to serve as goalposts)

▸ Timer

▸ Soccer ball

Setup

The player sets up the cones in a straight line, each 6 to 10 feet apart, at one end of the lawn. She sets up the soccer net at the opposite end of the lawn. (The cones are positioned to create a straight line leading toward the goal.)

Play

The player sets the stopwatch for 3 to 10 minutes. (Or the player simply does five repetitions of the drill, times herself, and does it again with the challenge to quicken her pace.) She places the soccer ball on the ground in the middle of the lawn and uses her feet to dribble the ball around each cone in the line. When she reaches the last cone, she dribbles around it and heads back toward the first cone, dribbling around each cone as she goes. When she gets back to her starting position, she dribbles so that she's clear of the cones and takes a shot at the goal. She then retrieves the ball, quickly dribbles back to the line of cones, and starts it all over again. She tries to complete as many runs and score as many goals as possible before the timer sounds.

61 DOUBLE-DRIBBLE

Your child plays the game at left, adding any of the three dribbling challenges below (listed in order from least to most difficult).

▶ Player uses the inside of her right foot to make two touches (taps to the ball) as she dribbles around the first cone, then switches to the inside of her left foot as she goes around the next cone. She continues alternating from one foot to the other.

▶ Player uses the inside of her right foot to make two touches as she dribbles around the first cone. She switches to the outside of her right foot as she dribbles around the next cone, continuing in this way and switching to the left foot on the next run.

▶ Player uses the outside of her right foot to make two touches as she dribbles around the first cone, then she uses the outside of the left foot, making two touches to dribble around the second cone, and so on, around each cone.

BASKETBALL CHALLENGE

AGE:
6–10 years

CATEGORY:
Solo Play/
Outdoor

**NUMBER OF
CHILDREN:**
One or more

*Use an adjustable basketball hoop and see what
kind of unique shot styles your child develops.*

Materials

▶ Sidewalk chalk

▶ Basketball or playground ball

▶ Adjustable basketball hoop

▶ Sports cones

Setup

Use the chalk to create a foul shot line on the
pavement.

Play

Your child can set up a series of solo challenges
for himself:

FOUL SHOTS Take 20 foul shots (from a standing
position, about 6 feet away) and score one point
for every shot that goes in.

BANK SHOTS Take 20 bank shots (a shot in
which the ball touches the backboard before
landing in the basket) and score one point for
each shot that goes in.

LAYUPS Do 20 layups (where you dribble up to
the basket and take the shot from up close) and
score one point for every shot that goes in.

DRIBBLE DRILL Set up sports cones in a straight line down the center of the pavement. Dribble the ball, circling around each cone in the line without stopping or dropping the ball. Repeat the drill, using your other hand.

TRICK SHOTS Create your own dribbling and shooting challenges and trick shots and use a small notepad to record how many shots or successful challenges were achieved each day. Set new challenges to beat your previous record.

A FEW DOLLARS WELL SPENT

PARENT TIP

"We bought our daughter a stopwatch from the sports store and she uses it to time herself during all sorts of games she plays outdoors. She has always enjoyed running and playing, but this simple tool has created hours of fun setting up challenges and playing ball games in our backyard."

—Larry from Colorado

WIFFLE GOLF HOLE IN ONE

AGE:
6–10 years

CATEGORY:
Solo Play/
Outdoor

**NUMBER OF
CHILDREN:**
One or more

Who needs a golf course when you've got a backyard and a Hula-Hoop?

Materials

▸ Large Hula-Hoop

▸ Golf tee

▸ Bucket of Wiffle golf balls

▸ Child-size plastic golf club

Setup

Place the Hula-Hoop at one end of the lawn and designate a shooting line at the other end by pressing a golf tee into the ground. (Place the Hula-Hoop close enough to the golf tee for your child to send balls into the hoop and experience the joy of succeeding with a bit of challenge thrown in for good measure.)

Play

Place a Wiffle ball on the tee. Your child will use the club to try to send the ball into the large hoop at the other end of the lawn to score a "hole in one." He keeps going until every ball in the bucket has been played and counts a point for every ball that lands inside the hoop.

65 FRISBEE TOSS HOLE IN ONE

This version of the game requires two Hula-Hoops and one Frisbee. The player places the hoops on the ground at opposite ends of the lawn. He stands inside one of the hoops, facing the hoop at the opposite end, and tosses the Frisbee toward the hoop, aiming to land it inside. He retrieves the Frisbee and goes to stand inside whichever hoop is closest and continues, scoring one point for every goal.

> "Mastery is this wonderful, exciting feeling: I'm better at it today than I was last week. It doesn't mean I'm the best in the world; it doesn't mean I won the Nobel Prize; it means simply: I'm getting better. I can do it better now than I could before—that is the root of motivation and self-esteem, and it's really magical."
>
> **—Edward Hallowell, MD**
> psychiatrist and author of
> *Driven to Distraction* and *CrazyBusy*

CLAPPING CALL-BALL

AGE:
6–10 years

CATEGORY:
Solo Play/
Outdoor

**NUMBER OF
CHILDREN:**
One or more

A simple challenge with clapping, throwing, catching, and the thrill of bouncing the ball higher and higher.

Materials

▸ Tennis ball or small rubber ball

Play

This should be played in a safe, grassy playing area free of obstacles. Your child tosses the ball into the air, calls out "one," and claps once before catching the ball. She tosses the ball a bit higher into the air, calls out "two," and claps twice before catching the ball. She continues tossing the ball and increasing the number of claps on each round of play, catching the ball after zero or one bounce.

67 BOUNCING CALL-BALL

Your child will need a bouncy rubber ball and access to a blacktop court. (A playground ball with lots of air works well, or for more of a challenge, she can use a smaller ball with lots of bounce.) She gives the ball a hard bounce on the pavement and sees how many times she can clap, attempting to catch it before it bounces on the pavement a second time. (The higher she can bounce the ball, the more claps she'll be able to fit in.)

FREE TIME FOR DAYDREAMING

Don't be fooled into thinking that nothing much is going on when you glance out the window and see your son swinging happily on the swing set. He may be dreaming up all sorts of good ideas—creating new lyrics for a popular song, inventing his own story about a fantasy character, or wondering about shapes in the clouds overhead. All this thinking, wondering, inventing, and creating are powerful parts of play. Children need time for unstructured play and daydreaming in their daily routine. Here are some outdoor play activities that provide opportunities to dream, invent, and create:

▸ Set up a tent and have a "campout" for a few hours.

▸ Build a fort, hideout, or lean-to with cardboard boxes.

▸ Draw designs (or a maze) on the sidewalk with chalk.

▸ Create roadways and a village in the sandbox.

▸ Skip stones across a pond or a lake.

▸ Have a spontaneous nature scavenger hunt outside.

▸ Use binoculars to watch birds and squirrels in the trees.

▸ Write letters and words in the sand at the beach.

▸ Sketch or draw in a peaceful place outside.

▸ Invent a fantasy team of your favorite baseball players.

▸ Gaze at the stars from the deck or backyard.

▸ Invent an obstacle course or a miniature-golf course.

▸ Look for a four-leaf clover.

▸ Chase fireflies on a summer evening.

STOOP-BALL

AGE:
6–10 years

CATEGORY:
Solo Play/
Outdoor

**NUMBER OF
CHILDREN:**
One or more

Playing Stoop-Ball alone is an excellent skill builder for tossing, catching, hand-eye coordination, and anticipating the ball's direction and timing.

Materials

▸ Tennis ball or small rubber ball

▸ Timer

Setup

The player finds a stoop (outdoor steps) not too close to a road.

Play

The player stands 4 feet or more away from the stoop and tosses the ball toward the steps, aiming to catch it as it bounces off one of the steps. Points are scored based on which part of the stoop the ball hits.

▸ If the ball hits in between two steps, score one point.

▸ If the ball bounces directly off the edge of a step, score 10 points.

▸ If the ball misses the stoop or the player doesn't catch it after one bounce, deduct one point.

The overall goal is for the player to score 100 points in a specific amount of time. To begin, set the timer or watch for 10 minutes and see if 100 points can be scored in this time. Adjust the timer to create a manageable challenge, given players' abilities and attention spans.

69 | A REAL SCAVENGER

AGE:
6–10 years

CATEGORY:
Solo Play/
Outdoor

**NUMBER OF
CHILDREN:**
One or more

* SAFETY ALERT

Supervise your child while she explores and teach her to identify anthills, hornet and wasp nests, poison ivy, poison oak, and snakes so she feels safe and confident exploring nature.

Nature holds a lot of buried and unburied treasures—find them!

Materials

▶ Paper

▶ Pencil

▶ Paper grocery bags

▶ Jars with holes in the lids

Setup

Make a list of items that can be found in nature: colorful stones, acorns, nuts, pine cones, pine needles, brilliant leaves, bark, bugs (take the jars with holes in the lids along for collecting), seed pods, flowers, worms, snails, twigs with interesting bumps and shapes, cattails, reeds, four-leaf clovers.

Play

Create a simple scavenger hunt for your child to have an outdoor adventure in your own backyard, neighborhood park, or playground. Have your child collect her finds in jars and paper bags, checking off items on her list (and adding some more, no doubt) as she explores.*

70 POINT IT OUT

Create a list of nature's treasures for your child to spot without collecting. In this case, you might include items you have spotted, such as spiderwebs, anthills, rotting tree stumps, or patches of clover.

TOYS TAKE A VACATION

PARENT TIP

"I realized one day that most of the toys my children had were not being played with on a regular basis. After many years of putting their toys away for them, I came up with the idea of 'vacation for toys.' It works like this: The children choose which toys will go in a box that eventually goes on vacation (storage). At first they were resistant, but finally they realized that everyone needs a vacation, even toys! After about six months, the toys come back from vacation and the kids are excited to have their old toys again. Now they enjoy sending their toys on vacation, and I enjoy having a room with less clutter and mess to clean up!"

—Wanda from Alaska

CHALLENGE!

Your child may see another child playing a game and think, "I wonder if I could do that." The desire to challenge oneself is a driving force for many solo games for kids all around the world. While organized sports may have a place in your child's routine, your child gains a unique sense of independence by simply going outside with a ball and "messing around on her own" to see what she can do.

BATTY-BIRD 100

AGE:
6–10 years

CATEGORY:
Solo Play/
Outdoor

**NUMBER OF
CHILDREN:**
One or more

This is a great game for a child who likes to test her focus; there's also some multitasking involved.

Materials

▸ Badminton racket

▸ Birdie (officially called a shuttlecock)

Play

This game should be played on a flat lawn. The player holds the racket so that the netting is parallel to the ground and uses it to tap the birdie continuously, sending it about a foot up into the air each time. The player tries to get to 50 continuous taps; if the birdie slips off the racket, she must start all over again. When the player gets to 51 taps, the difficulty of the game increases, and the birdie gets tapped higher into the air, about 3 feet above the racket. When the player reaches 75 taps, she increases the power of her taps again, sending the birdie even higher into the air (8 to 10 feet). The aim is to get to 100 taps. (At the third level, catching the birdie is likely to involve some running around the lawn.)

BEANBAG TARGET TOSS

AGE:
6–10 years

CATEGORY:
Solo Play/
Outdoor

**NUMBER OF
CHILDREN:**
One or more

*A perfect after-school game for a child who needs
to burn off a little steam after sitting at a desk
all day.*

Materials

▸ Sidewalk chalk
▸ Timer
▸ Beanbags

Setup

Your child draws a large chalk circle on the
sidewalk or pavement, then draws straight
lines inside the circle to create four, six, or
eight slices of the pie. He assigns a specific
number of points to each slice, then uses the
chalk to draw a pitching line several feet away.

Play

Your child stands behind the pitching line
and sets the timer for 5 minutes or more, then
begins pitching beanbags into the pie slices,
scoring points accordingly. (No points are
scored when the beanbag lands on a dividing
line or outside the circle.) He tries to score
50 points before the buzzer sounds.

DOUBLE CHALLENGE

Create a second pitching line several feet
behind the original one with the option of
scoring double points by throwing from the
farthest line. Move back and forth between
the two to vary the level of challenge.

75 BULL'S-EYE

Your child adds a smaller circle (bull's-eye) in the center of the pie. He scores 10 or more points for a bull's-eye.

76 JUMP ROPE

AGE:
6–10 years

CATEGORY:
Solo Play/
Outdoor

**NUMBER OF
CHILDREN:**
One or more

* SAFETY ALERT

Make sure your child wears athletic shoes. Sandals, flip-flops, or shoes with buckles can catch on the rope and increase the risk of injury.

Children love to get really good at jumping rope on their own so they can wow their friends on the playground with their smooth moves.

Materials

▶ Jump rope

▶ Sidewalk or other paved playing surface

▶ Timer

CLASSIC ACTIVITY

Play*

After your child has gotten comfortable with the rhythm of using a jump rope, here are some challenges she can set for herself to make things more interesting:

LEFT-RIGHT Skip on one foot, alternating feet with every skip.

LONG HOPPER Skip on one foot for as long as you can, then switch to the other.

HOPPER TIME Set the timer and count how many times you can jump in 3 minutes, 4 minutes, or 5 minutes.

2
PARENT & CHILD PLAY

ay "yes" to "Will you play with me?" whenever possible. Time with your child is all about doing—moving, thinking, guessing, and creating. Children six to ten are keen observers who pick up nuances of skill, strategy, and technique. So, without much fanfare (and perhaps few words), your child is absorbing, learning, and expanding because he is playing with you. And play can also bring out amazing questions or comments from your six-to-ten-year-old that let you know what he's thinking, what he's imagining, or even what he's concerned about. Here are some games to play and crafts to make on those happy days when you say "yes" to playing together.

> 66
>
> It's very interesting that some of the most important studies we have on creativity show that adults who still retain that capacity to play, to think up new ways to use objects or to play games—just original thinking of any kind—these are the people who, as adults, really get ahead. And that creativity begins in childhood."
>
> **—Jane M. Healy, PhD**
> educational psychologist and author of *Your Child's Growing Mind* and *Failure to Connect: How Computers Affect Our Children's Minds*

INDOOR PLAY

Parents are terrific at multitasking, so guessing and word games can easily be played together while you are chopping veggies or stirring the stew. (Or play in the car when you're driving across town.)

77 ## RHYMING RIDDLES

AGE:
6–10 years

CATEGORY:
Parent & Child/
Indoor

**NUMBER OF
CHILDREN:**
One or more

There's a rhythm to playing this game, and once your child gets it, he'll create loads of quick mismatched sentences for you to figure out.

Play

Think of a sentence with familiar words, like "I went to the park and played on the slide." Now say this sentence out loud, substituting rhyming words for one or more of the words in the sentence; you might say, "I went to the park and played on the *Clyde*." Your child tries to guess the correct word or words in the original sentence. (Inflect the mismatched word to let your child know which word is out of sync.) After a few rounds of play, give your child a chance to create sentences while you take a turn guessing. (Provide pencil and paper so your child can write down the original sentence and experiment with rhyming words on paper before announcing his Rhyming Riddle.)

GOING ON A PICNIC

AGE:
6–10 years

CATEGORY:
Parent & Child/
Indoor

**NUMBER OF
CHILDREN:**
One or more

This game is terrific to play on long car trips or to pass the time while waiting in the doctor's office.

Setup

Select one player to begin the game.

Play

One child begins by saying, "I'm going on a picnic and I'm bringing _____" (*insert the name of a picnic item that begins with the letter* A). The second player repeats this statement the same way and then adds on: "I'm also bringing _____" (*insert item beginning with the letter* B). As the game moves on through the letters of the alphabet, each child must remember all the items previously mentioned. When a child stumbles and cannot remember an item in the list, she starts the game over, beginning with the letter A. (If you prefer to keep score, mark a point each time a player gets through the entire list of items correctly and adds one new item with the next letter of the alphabet. The child with the most points wins.) Keep in mind that there are plenty of nonfood items to bring to a picnic!

CONCENTRATION

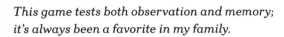

AGE:
6–10 years

CATEGORY:
Parent & Child/
Indoor

**NUMBER OF
CHILDREN:**
One or more

*This game tests both observation and memory;
it's always been a favorite in my family.*

Materials

▸ Deck of playing cards with matching pairs (a standard
deck, Go Fish deck, or Animal Rummy deck)

Setup

Shuffle the deck of cards and lay them out
(no piles) on the floor or table, facedown in
a rectangular configuration.

Play

Players must try to remember the position of
each card they see turned over. The first player
turns over any two cards in the rectangle,
looking to match the numbers, face cards (jack,
queen, king), or animals. If the cards match,
she removes these two cards (putting them
in her "pile") and turns over two more cards,
looking for another match. If the cards do
not match, they are returned to their original
facedown positions and the next person takes
a turn. At first, she'll be turning cards over at
random, but soon she'll have built up enough
of a memory bank to make matches by going
back to cards she's seen turned over. The game
continues until all the matches have been
made. Each player counts the cards in her pile,
and the player with the most cards wins.

WHAT WOULD YOU INVENT?

NOTE

If your child likes the idea of being an inventor, here's a good book to enjoy together: *So You Want to Be an Inventor?* by Judith St. George, illustrations by David Small.

Here's a way to tap into your child's creative thinking abilities.

Play

Create a list of real-life places and ask, "What gadget would you invent to make things easier or better in/on (*insert the name of the place*)?" For example: "What gadget would you invent to make a barn better for cows?" This simple question starts some marvelous ideas flowing with many twists and turns. Other familiar places might include:

▸ The kitchen

▸ The school cafeteria

▸ The soccer or baseball field

▸ The train or subway station

▸ The highway

▸ An airplane

▸ A car or truck

▸ A farm

▸ The garage

▸ The doctor's office

▸ An office

▸ A restaurant

▸ The post office

▸ The grocery store

▸ The ocean

HOUSE RULES

"My six-year-old knows that we have 'house rules' concerning playing. Most of these rules involve safety or playing fair. We simply mention a 'house rule' on an as-needed basis when we see him doing something unsafe or when he pushes to do something that he knows is off-limits. What we've noticed is that he often passes these house rules along to the other kids when they come over to play. Recently I overheard him say, 'My dad says we can't leave the backyard, that's one of our house rules,' when a playmate suggested they go down to the schoolyard to play. It's an easy way to talk about what's okay and what is not okay, and also it gives him a way to save face if a friend suggests something he knows is not allowed in our family."

—Michael from Ohio

If a child is bored, that means that they're having some time to sit and think, 'What can I do next?' and that's a valuable skill."

—Maureen O'Brien, PhD
child development specialist and author of
Watch Me Grow: I'm One-Two-Three

TIC-TAC-TOE

AGE:
6–10 years

CATEGORY:
Parent & Child/
Indoor

**NUMBER OF
CHILDREN:**
One or more

*It's hard to imagine a world without tic-tac-toe.
It seems like this game has been around since
the dawn of time....*

Materials

▶ Paper

▶ Pencil

Setup

Draw a simple grid with two vertical lines
and two horizontal lines intersecting them.
(Leave an inch between each of these lines to
allow players to fit Xs and Os into the squares
created by the grid.)

Play

One player chooses *X* as his mark and the
other chooses *O*. Toss a coin to see which
player goes first. The first player then puts
his mark in one of the squares on the grid.
(The middle square is the best bet for the
first mark!) The second player puts one mark
down. Each player continues filling in his *X*
or *O* with the goal of getting three marks in
a row, horizontally, vertically, or diagonally.
If neither player is successful getting three
marks in a row, the round is considered a
"draw" and a new game begins.

83 ## DESERT ISLAND

AGE:
6–10 years

CATEGORY:
Parent & Child/
Indoor

**NUMBER OF
CHILDREN:**
One or more

**QUICK
& EASY**

*The desert-island question often leads to lively
debate, with everyone adamantly defending
their tastes.*

Materials

▸ Small notepad

▸ Pencil

Play

"If you were stranded on a desert island,
what ten items would you really want to take
with you?" You pose the question, and your
child writes his list on a piece of paper. See
if you can guess what's on his list. Mix it up
for the second round of play, with your child
posing the question while you write down your
favorite can't-do-without-it things, and see if
your child can use what he knows about you
to guess what's on your list.

84 ### TEN FOODS

"What ten *foods* would you take with you on a
desert island?"

85 ### FAMILY FAVORITES

Pick a category of foods, such as dessert, ice-
cream flavors, breakfast foods, or restaurant
dishes. Each player writes down his five or
ten favorite items and the rest of the family
guesses what favorite foods each person has
on their list.

FRIENDSHIP

Play is a natural way for children to develop strong social skills and fine-tune their emotional intelligence. Whether your child prefers one best friend or moves easily among many friends, friendship matters. If you ask a six-year-old boy or girl what he or she does with friends, you get variations of the same answer: "We play!"

Here's a quick look at some of the excellent ways your child can grow and learn while playing with friends:

▸ He learns that each friend has different wants, needs, feelings, and interests, distinctly different from his own.

▸ She learns to cooperate, take turns, and negotiate.

▸ He discovers that he can say or do something to help a friend. He can cheer them up, make them laugh, or lend a helping hand. His words and actions can make a difference to others.

▸ She realizes that there are times when she has to speak up for herself or for what she feels is right.

▸ He has a chance to practice managing emotions—anger, frustration, impatience.

▸ She learns that she can bounce back after experiencing teasing or rejection from another child.

▸ He understands the value of trust and loyalty.

▸ She learns to take responsibility for hurting someone's feelings and learns how to apologize.

DID YOU KNOW?

AGE:
6–10 years

CATEGORY:
Parent & Child/
Indoor

**NUMBER OF
CHILDREN:**
One or more

*This splendid storytelling game encourages
kids and parents to weave the most outlandish
tall tales.*

Play

Find an object in the room and tell a spontaneous
tall tale about it. The more outlandish, the
better—"Did you know that that purple car
outside was once driven by an elephant who
was in a rush to get to his doctor's appointment?
He hit his big toe with a hammer when he
was building a special slide for his friend the
giraffe. His toe swelled up like a balloon, and
he couldn't fit his foot into his shoe, so he had
to come to the doctor's office barefoot!" Each
player takes a turn telling a tall tale about
any object within their field of vision. (At the
end of each tale, I like to show respect for the
storyteller by announcing, "I did NOT know
that" with great fanfare.)

AGE:
6–10 years

CATEGORY:
Parent & Child/
Indoor

**NUMBER OF
CHILDREN:**
One

Who needs Wheel of Fortune? *This classic word game is fun for adults and kids and can be played whenever and wherever there's pencil and paper.*

Materials

▶ Paper
▶ Pencil

Play

One player will be the Hangman for the first round of play. The Hangman thinks of a word and marks a row of blank dashes on the paper, one dash for every letter of the mystery word. The other player tries to guess a letter in the mystery word. If she guesses incorrectly, the Hangman draws the first line of her "gallows"—the base. She also writes the incorrect guess on the paper as a reminder not to guess it again. If she guesses correctly, the Hangman fills in the appropriate blank, and she can choose to take a guess at the mystery word. If she guesses the mystery word, she beats the Hangman and becomes the new Hangman. If the Hangman completes her drawing before anyone guesses the word, she wins that round of play and takes a second turn at being Hangman.

88 | I SPY

AGE:
6–10 years

CATEGORY:
Parent & Child/
Indoor

**NUMBER OF
CHILDREN:**
One or more

*A quick eye and a quick mouth are all you need
to play this game.*

Play

One player is elected as the spy. The spy fixes
on a particular object within his field of vision,
either indoors or out. The spy says, "I spy with
my little eye, something that begins with the
letter ___ ." The other players look around the
room and call out guesses as fast as they can:
"Is it a banana?" "A bowl?" "A bottle?" The spy
answers no, not giving away any other hints,
until someone guesses correctly. The person
who guesses the correct object becomes the
next spy.

89 | INVISIBLE WORDS

AGE:
6–10 years

CATEGORY:
Parent & Child/
Indoor

**NUMBER OF
CHILDREN:**
One or more

No pencil and paper needed for this writing game!

Play

Using your finger, outline one letter at a time
on your child's back to create an invisible
word. When you are finished, your child takes
a guess. If the guess is correct, she trades
places and writes a word on your back. (If she
guesses incorrectly, write the word again and
let her take another guess.)

90 PICTURE PERFECT

Rather than writing, try outlining a simple shape—the sun, a tree, a rocket ship—on your child's back and let the guessing game begin!

91 WHAT'S THAT YOU'RE EATING?

AGE:
6–10 years

CATEGORY:
Parent & Child/
Indoor

NUMBER OF CHILDREN:
One or more

This simplified version of charades is always good for a few laughs.

Play

The first player thinks of a food and silently pretends to eat this particular food without props of any kind. The other players guess at what the food is. The wide range of possible pantomimes can make things very interesting. Think of peeling an orange, slicing an apple, picking up one shelled peanut at a time, dipping chicken fingers in honey-mustard sauce or french fries in ketchup, or eating a hamburger. Everyone takes a turn acting out eating a particular food while the others do the guessing.

KITCHEN-TABLE PLAY

Although children six to ten years old are much more independent than preschoolers, they still enjoy the comfort of playing alongside Mom or Dad. With these kitchen activities, I've also included some thinking and guessing games that your child can either play with you as you work nearby or play alone (with pencil and paper to jot down guesses).

92 WINDOW WAGER

AGE:
6–10 years

CATEGORY:
Parent & Child/
Indoor

**NUMBER OF
CHILDREN:**
One or more

It all started with a piece of paper, a pencil, and a wager. . . .

Materials
▶ Pencils
▶ Paper
▶ Notepad

Play
The game begins with a question like "How many windows are in our home?" (Other items you might place wagers on are doorknobs, lightbulbs, framed photos or paintings, and shoes.) Each player quickly writes down a guess on a piece of paper and folds it in half without the other player seeing it. Give your child a notepad and pencil and let her be the Auditor who sets out to discover whose guess comes closest.

93 CLASS COUNT

AGE:
6–10 years

CATEGORY:
Parent & Child/
Indoor

**NUMBER OF
CHILDREN:**
One or more

*Test your child's observation skills with this fun
way to get her talking about school.*

Materials

▸ Paper
▸ Pencil

Play

Challenge your child to write down or call out
the name of every child in her class, giving
one detail about what each classmate likes to
do, play, wear, eat, say, etc.

KITCHEN-TABLE PLAY CLASSICS

▸ Cat's Cradle string game
▸ Dominoes
▸ Etch A Sketch
▸ Jacks
▸ LEGOs
▸ Models (planes, boats, cars)

▸ Pick-up Sticks
▸ Puzzles
▸ Rush Hour
▸ Solitaire
▸ Squeezed Out
▸ Yo-yo

LOST AND FOUND

AGE:
6–10 years

CATEGORY:
Parent & Child/
Indoor

**NUMBER OF
CHILDREN:**
One or more

Quick searching skills and nimble fingers win out in this kitchen table game.

Materials

▸ Paper and pencil

▸ Magazines with lots of photos

▸ Timer

Setup

Suggest 10 to 20 items that might be found in the pages of a magazine, and have your child make a list of these items. Some items should be common and others more challenging. Common examples might include a dog, a cat, a dinner plate, fruit, vegetables, shoes, a baby, eyeglasses, or jewelry. Challenging items might include a red car, a barbecue grill, yellow flowers, a boat, a hammer, a lawn chair, a fence, or a motorcycle.

Play

Set the timer for 10 to 15 minutes. Your child begins searching through the magazines for each item on the list. When an item is found, she tears the page from the magazine and/or checks it off the list. Once the timer sounds, add up the number of items found in the magazine.

WHAT'S COOKING?

AGE:
6–10 years

CATEGORY:
Parent & Child/
Indoor

**NUMBER OF
CHILDREN:**
One or more

*A terrific way for younger children to practice
spelling, vocabulary, and pronunciation, as you
try to guess the mystery recipe.*

Materials

▸ A basic cookbook

▸ Large rubber bands

Setup

The two sections of the cookbook to be used
for this game are Main Dishes and Desserts.
Use the rubber bands to parcel off the unneeded
sections of the cookbook to make it easier to
navigate.

Play

Your child selects one familiar recipe from
the Main Dishes or Desserts section of the
cookbook. He announces the category (either
main dish or dessert), and then reads any one
ingredient in the recipe to get the guessing
game started. For example, if the selected
recipe is beef stew, he would reveal that the
category is a "main dish" and perhaps give
the first clue ingredient as "celery." You can
then either take a wild guess on that first clue
or simply say, "More clues, please." Your child
continues offering ingredients as clues until
you make a correct guess or give up and ask
for the correct answer.

96   **DICTIONARY DETECTIVE**

AGE:
6–10 years

CATEGORY:
Parent & Child/
Indoor

**NUMBER OF
CHILDREN:**
One or more

NOTE

This game is
best suited for
children with
reasonably good
reading and
spelling skills.

*A fun challenge that has the added benefit of
putting the dictionary into frequent circulation.*

Materials

▸ Children's dictionary

Play

Your child flips the dictionary open to any
page, selects a word of his choice, and, without
saying the word, reads the definition out loud.
You (or another player) must try to guess the
mystery word described after hearing the
definition.

97   SPELLING BEE

In this variation, you select a page in the
dictionary and find one word on that page
that your child must try to spell. Or pass the
dictionary to your child and let your child
select challenging words for *you* to spell
correctly.

I'M THINKING OF A FOOD . . .

AGE:
6–10 years

CATEGORY:
Parent & Child/
Indoor

**NUMBER OF
CHILDREN:**
One or more

Your child tries to stump you by offering a series of clues about a mystery food.

Materials

▸ Garden seed catalog (printed in color)

Play

Your child starts the game by thinking of a specific food found in a seed catalog, such as a pineapple, and offering a series of clues about this food that follow the specific order listed below (the clues progress from least revealing to most revealing):

1. Any one letter found in the name of the mystery food

2. The color of the food

3. The shape of the food

4. The texture of the food

5. The category of the food (fruit, vegetable, or grain)

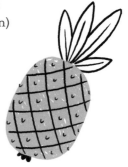

READING ALOUD

Even though they can read on their own, children still get tremendous pleasure and comfort from listening as you read to them. And reading aloud to the six- to ten-year-old crowd often happens to be the one kind of play that a busy, tired parent can manage at the end of a long day! Here are a few of my favorite books for children six to ten years old. Please keep in mind that some of these books may be too "old" for your particular child, while others may seem too "young." There's a wide range of individual preferences and interests within this age group, so use what you know about your child to select a book that is just right.

PICTURE BOOKS

Amelia Bedelia
by Peggy Parish,
illustrations
by Fritz Siebel

Arthur series
by Marc Brown

The Story of Babar:
The Little Elephant
by Jean De Brunhoff

A Birthday for Frances
by Russell Hoban,
illustrations
by Lillian Hoban

The Cat in the Hat
by Dr. Seuss

Chester's Way
by Kevin Henkes

Cloudy with a Chance
of Meatballs
by Judi Barrett,
illustrations
by Ron Barrett

Doctor DeSoto
by William Steig

Double Trouble
in Walla Walla
by Andrew Clements,
illustrations by
Salvatore Murdocca

> One thing I encourage parents to do is turn off the car radio, turn off the headsets and computer games, and just talk. Tell stories, talk about the events of the day, have 'what if' conversations. What if you were walking down the street and saw a bag full of money, what would be the best thing to do?"
>
> **—Mary Pipher, PhD**
> psychotherapist and author of
> *Reviving Ophelia* and *The Shelter of Each Other*

Eloise
by Kay Thompson, illustrations by Hilary Knight

Green Eggs and Ham
by Dr. Seuss

Henry and Mudge and the Great Grandpas
by Cynthia Rylant, illustrations by Sucie Stevenson

Little Bear by Else Holmelund Minarik, illustrations by Maurice Sendak

Martha Speaks by Susan Meddaugh

Miss Nelson Is Missing!, *Miss Nelson Is Back*, and *Miss Nelson Has a Field Day* by Harry Allard

Nate the Great
by Marjorie Weinman Sharmat, illustrations by Marc Simont

Once There Was a Bull . . . (Frog) by Rick Walton

One Fish, Two Fish, Red Fish, Blue Fish
by Dr. Seuss

Peter's Chair by Ezra Jack Keats

Terrific by Jon Agee

The Polar Express
by Chris Van Allsburg

The Stinky Cheese Man and Other Fairly Stupid Tales by Jon Scieszka, illustrations by Lane Smith

Traction Man Is Here
by Mini Grey

CHAPTER BOOKS

Captain Underpants
by Dav Pilkey

American Girl Collection (series)

Babe: The Gallant Pig
by Dick King-Smith

A Bear Called Paddington
by Michael Bond, illustrations by Peggy Fortnum

The Best Christmas Pageant Ever
by Barbara Robinson

Charlie and the Chocolate Factory
by Roald Dahl, illustrations by Quentin Blake

Charlotte's Web
by E. B. White, illustrations by Garth Williams

The Cricket in Times Square
by George Selden, illustrations by Garth Williams

Frog and Toad Are Friends (and others in the series) by Arnold Lobel

Harriet the Spy
by Louise Fitzhugh

Harry Potter and the Sorcerer's Stone
by J. K. Rowling

I would set firm limits on screen time. That means a limited number of hours per week and choice of programs to be determined with the parent. For school-age kids, homework is more important, play is more important, activities are more important; and the television needs to be secondary to all those things."

—Jane M. Healy, PhD
educational psychologist and author of
Your Child's Growing Mind and *Failure to Connect: How Computers Affect Our Children's Minds*

James and the Giant Peach by Roald Dahl, illustrations by Lane Smith

Little House on the Prairie by Laura Ingalls Wilder, illustrations by Garth Williams

Miracle at the Plate (and other sports classics) by Matt Christopher

The Mouse and the Motorcycle by Beverly Cleary

Mr. Popper's Penguins by Richard Atwater

Mrs. Piggle-Wiggle by Betty MacDonald, illustrations by Alexandra Boiger

Ramona Forever by Beverly Cleary, illustrations by Jacqueline Rogers

Ramona Quimby, Age 8 by Beverly Cleary, illustrations by Jacqueline Rogers

Ramona the Pest by Beverly Cleary, illustrations by Jacqueline Rogers

Sarah Plain and Tall by Patricia MacLachlan

The Secret Garden by Frances Hodgson Burnett

Stuart Little by E. B. White

REFERENCE BOOKS
(VALUABLE RESOURCES FOR AD–LIB GAMES):

Merriam-Webster Children's Dictionary

National Geographic Kids World Atlas

Children's Encyclopedia of Animals

Oxford's Children's Rhyming Dictionary

CRAFT ACTIVITIES

Some of the best children's crafts are made from inexpensive, everyday materials. A few scraps of yarn, a shoelace or two, a box of macaroni, or an ordinary shoebox may be all you need to get things started. Rummage through the house to round up your materials, place newspapers (or an old tablecloth) over the kitchen table to designate your craft corner, and you're heading in the right direction. Here are some ideas that allow your child to transform these ho-hum ingredients into something clever, creative, and original with a little help from you.

99 DRIP-DROP POSTCARDS

AGE:
6–10 years

CATEGORY:
Parent & Child/
Indoor

**NUMBER OF
CHILDREN:**
One or more

These postcards are colorful and truly unique works of art, though they are created quite simply. (What's more, you can make 45 postcards from one sheet of matte board, so they are quite inexpensive to make.)

Materials

▶ Yardstick

▶ Pencil

▶ Scissors

▶ 32-inch-by-40-inch sheet of matte board

▶ Washable paints

▶ Disposable foil muffin tin

▶ Plastic eyedroppers (1 for each print color)

▶ Fine-tip marker

Setup

Using the yardstick, pencil, and scissors, mark and cut up 4-inch-by-6-inch postcards from the large sheet of matte board. (You can make 45 postcards from one sheet of matte board!) Pour a small quantity of each color of paint into the compartments of the muffin tin. Lay out one eyedropper for each color of paint.

Create

You and your child work with two postcards each; place the cards textured (matte) side up on the table. Dip the end of one of the eyedroppers into the paint and squeeze the bulb until the dropper is full of paint. Carefully and quickly place this eyedropper over one of the postcards and squeeze to release small circles of color onto the postcard. Select another color of paint and, using a clean eyedropper, repeat the same process on this first card. Continue adding additional colors of paint drops in random designs or controlled shapes or letters. (Overlap some of the drops to create different colors altogether.) Pick up the second, blank postcard and gently place it matte side down over the paint-drop card. Use your hand to apply some pressure to the card "sandwich." Gently pry the cards apart and place them faceup on the table to dry. Once they're thoroughly dry, turn them over and use a fine-tip marker to draw a vertical line down their center. Now you've got a postcard!

PAPIER-MÂCHÉ MASKS

AGE:
6–10 years

CATEGORY:
Parent & Child/
Indoor

**NUMBER OF
CHILDREN:**
One or more

* SAFETY ALERT

Supervise all
balloon play to
prevent children
less than eight
years old from
choking on
uninflated
balloons or
balloon pieces.

*This project is excellent for children with a little
prior papier-mâché experience and a flair for
creative details.*

Materials

▶ Newspaper or recycled
vinyl tablecloth

▶ Papier-mâché goop (see
recipe on opposite page)

▶ Newsprint paper

▶ Scissors

▶ Large balloon*
(to make 2 masks)

▶ Large plastic
margarine tub

▶ Duct tape

▶ Cookie sheet

▶ Safety pin

▶ Washable paint or
nontoxic poster paint

▶ Yarn, ribbon, feathers,
fabric, etc.

▶ Single-hole punch

Setup

Cover your kitchen table with newspapers.
Make the goop, let it cool, and place a large
bowl of it on the table. Tear or cut newsprint into
1-inch-by-6-inch strips. Tear a large quantity
before proceeding to the messy part of this project.
Blow up the balloon and tie it off. Place the knotted
end of the inflated balloon inside the margarine
tub and secure the bottom of the balloon to the tub
with duct tape. Place the margarine tub and balloon
on the cookie sheet.

Create

Dip a newsprint strip into the bowl of goop, making
sure it is completely covered. Pull the strip out,
holding it over the goop bowl, and smooth off any

excess goop by sliding your index and middle fingers down the length of the paper strip. Place this strip around the balloon. Repeat this process until the entire balloon is covered with about four layers of goopy paper strips. Allow three to four days for it to dry completely. (Drying time may vary.) Pop the balloon with a safety pin. Insert scissors at the bottom of the oval and cut the balloon-shaped paper creation in half lengthwise to create two masks. You can help your child cut out eyes and a mouth opening, or simply draw eyes, nose, and lips with paints and markers. Decorate with paint, glitter, glue, yarn, feathers, etc. Punch holes on each side of your masks (by the ears) and tie ribbons through the holes, knotting them off on the inside of the masks. Tie the ribbons in a bow to hang this artwork on the wall or tie them to fit your child's head.

PAPIER-MÂCHÉ GOOP

2 cups cold water

½ cup flour

2 cups boiling water

4 tablespoons sugar

Stir the cold water and flour together in a bowl, blending well to dissolve all lumps. Pour 2 cups of water into a saucepan and bring to a boil. Add the cold water and flour mixture to the saucepan, stirring constantly, and bring to a boil. Remove from heat and stir in the sugar. Let this mixture cool.

PAPIER-MÂCHÉ BOWL

AGE:
6–10 years

CATEGORY:
Parent & Child/
Indoor

**NUMBER OF
CHILDREN:**
One or more

* SAFETY ALERT

Supervise
all balloon
play to prevent
children less
than eight years
old from choking
on uninflated
balloons or
balloon pieces.

CLASSIC
ACTIVITY

*There is something almost indescribable about
the pleasure of getting your hands in slippery
papier-mâché goop. It's messy, and the goop takes
days to dry. And that's part of the appeal.*

Materials

▸ Papier-mâché goop
(see recipe on
page 111)

▸ Newspaper or recycled
vinyl tablecloth

▸ Newsprint paper

▸ Scissors

▸ Medium balloon*

▸ Felt-tipped marker

▸ Large plastic
margarine tub
or bowl

▸ Duct tape

▸ Cookie sheet

▸ Safety pin

▸ Washable paint
or nontoxic
poster paint

▸ Paintbrush

Setup

Make the goop and let it cool. Cover your
kitchen table with newspapers. Place a large
bowl of goop on the table. Tear or cut newsprint
pages into strips about 1 inch wide and 6 inches
long. (It's best to tear a large quantity of these
strips before proceeding to the messy part
of this project.) Blow up the balloon and tie it
off. Use the marker to draw a line all the way
around the balloon, about halfway up from the
bottom. (You'll be using the balloon as a mold
for the bowl, and your child will be lining up
newsprint strips along this marker.) Place the
knotted end of the inflated balloon inside the

You may use
newspaper
instead of
newsprint, but
painting over
the black ink
can be a bit of
a challenge.

This is a
decorative
bowl and is not
intended for
holding food of
any kind.

margarine tub and secure the bottom of the
balloon to the tub with strips of duct tape. Place
the margarine tub (with balloon attached) on
the cookie sheet to catch any drips while you
work and while the project dries.

Create

Dip a newsprint strip into the bowl of goop,
making sure it is completely covered. Pull the
strip out, holding it over the goop bowl, and
smooth off any excess goop by sliding your
index and middle fingers down the length of the
paper strip. Place this strip around the balloon.
Add more strips until you've completely
covered the balloon up to the "stop line." Now
begin to layer, applying four layers of strips.
Use your hands to smooth out each strip so that
it doesn't have huge bumps or lumps (but don't
go crazy here—the finished bowl will have a
handmade texture, which adds to its beauty).

Allow the bowl three or four days to dry
completely (drying time may vary depending
on your climate and humidity level). Once the
newspaper is dry, pop the balloon with the
safety pin and decorate the bowl with paints.

ECO BEADS

AGE:
6–10 years

CATEGORY:
Parent & Child/
Indoor

**NUMBER OF
CHILDREN:**
One or more

A green parent's dream—recycling magazines destined for the dump and unleashing your child's creative spirit!

Materials

▸ Colored pages from magazines

▸ Scissors

▸ Pencil

▸ Nontoxic white glue

▸ String, yarn, or dental floss

Create

1. You and your child cut large and small triangles from colorful magazine photos.

2. Roll a paper triangle tightly around a pencil.

3. When you have nearly rolled the entire triangle, place a dab of glue on the point of the triangle still left sticking out, then roll it tightly in and hold in place a few seconds to let the glue begin to set.

4. Slide the bead off the pencil and allow the glue to continue to dry.

5. String these assorted beads on string or yarn, knotting the ends of the string together to create a long necklace that can be easily slipped on and off.

103 JAGGED ECO BEADS

Use thin sheets of colored paper or tissue paper
to create the triangles. Roll as described above,
but leave a half-inch of the paper point dangling.
Glue the rolled paper at the last point of contact
and hold for a few seconds to let the glue dry.
This creates a varied bead with ragged edges.
After letting these beads dry completely, string
them on the yarn to create a necklace.

> " With television it's so easy to become a passive
> viewer of other people's ideas and other people's
> lives instead of becoming the creator of your own
> life and your own ideas."
>
> **—T. A. Barron**
> author of The Lost Years series

104 PERSONALIZED TREASURE BOX

AGE:
6–10 years

CATEGORY:
Parent & Child/
Indoor

NUMBER OF CHILDREN:
One or more

Children love to have a special place for treasured keepsakes; these boxes take on added value over time, so be sure to keep them somewhere safe.

Materials

▸ Nontoxic white glue

▸ Disposable foil pie pan

▸ Small shoebox or chocolate box with lid

▸ Pasta in various shapes (wheels, macaroni, ziti, shells, etc.)

▸ Paintbrushes

▸ Poster paint

Create

Pour glue into the pie pan and add a little water to make it more spreadable. Spread a generous layer of glue on the shoebox lid and decorate with pasta pieces. (If you or your child are working slowly or creating an elaborate design, put glue on only one section of the lid at a time so it doesn't dry out before you've done the sticking.) Paint the sides of the box with poster paint, embellish with drawings and designs, and be sure to allow a bit of space for your child's name and age. If your child is willing to go the extra mile, decorating the sides of the box with strips of fabric is also a nice finishing touch.

105 BUTTON TREASURE BOX

Decorate the lid with buttons to create a colorful design or to spell out your child's name.

OUTDOOR PLAY

What can be better than heading outdoors on a warm, sunny day to play with your child? You might join in because you know your child enjoys this outdoor playtime, but chances are that you too will reap many benefits and build memories of your own. (And don't be shy about taking a trip down memory lane to recall some of *your* favorite childhood games. Chances are, if it was a fun game for you many years ago, it will be a fun game to play with your child now. Perennial favorites like catch, Frisbee toss, and croquet absolutely never go out of style.) Here are some game suggestions that celebrate the joy of playing together in the great outdoors.

106 NEIGHBORHOOD NUMBER TRAIL

AGE:
6–10 years

CATEGORY:
Parent & Child/
Outdoor

**NUMBER OF
CHILDREN:**
One

Celebrate the simple pleasure of an afternoon walk—turned into a mathematical scavenger hunt where numbers lurk around every corner.

Materials
▸ Pencil
▸ Paper

Setup
Walk down your block or around your neighborhood without your child and create a list of clues about 10 things in your neighborhood that have a number attached to them—"The number of stones around

Mrs. Johnson's mailbox," for example. Write these clues on lined paper, skipping lines for answers and leaving room at the bottom for the grand total.

Play

Give your child the list of clues you made and set off on a walk together around the neighborhood. (Remember to bring a pencil and follow the same route that you traveled while making your list.) Your child reads each clue, figures out what number the clue refers to, and writes that number on the list. (Give additional tips and clues as needed along the way.) Once you're back inside, add up all the numbers to come up with a grand total, the Neighborhood Number of the day.

107 THE MAGIC NUMBER IS . . .

This is a terrific game for family walks. Let your child pick a number from 10 to 20. As you walk, hunt through the neighborhood for the magic number. Look on mailboxes, license plates, phone numbers painted on trucks and vans, house numbers, and anywhere else you can think of. Carry a small notepad and pencil to keep track of how many magic numbers were found.

HORSE

AGE:
6–10 years

CATEGORY:
Parent & Child/
Outdoor

**NUMBER OF
CHILDREN:**
Two or more

*Children always love games that look like
grown-up sports, and here's one that can easily
be modified to fit your child's age and abilities.*

Materials

▸ Adjustable basketball hoop

▸ Playground ball or basketball

Setup

Set the basketball goal (hoop and net) at the
right height for the players. Toss a coin to see
which player goes first.

Play

The first player takes a shot at the basket from
anywhere on the court or pavement. If she
doesn't make a basket, she earns an *H* (the
first letter of the word *horse*) as a penalty, and
the second player takes a turn. If she does
make the basket, the second player must stand
in the exact same spot as she did for his shot.
If the second player misses the shot, he earns
an *H*. The game continues this way, with the
letters progressing through the word *horse*.
The first player to collect all the letters in the
word *horse* loses.

BEANBAG HORSESHOES

AGE:
6–10 years

CATEGORY:
Parent & Child/
Outdoor

**NUMBER OF
CHILDREN:**
Two or more

Here's a kid-friendly variation of the old favorite.

Materials

▸ Hula-Hoop

▸ Beanbags

▸ Roll of 2-inch-wide painter's tape

Setup

Mark start and finish lines by placing 6-foot-long strips of tape on the grass. (Roll out the tape, sticky side down, in 12-inch sections, pressing it down with your feet as you go.) Place the Hula-Hoop on the ground near the finish line.

Play

Each player stands behind the start line and gets three turns tossing beanbags inside the hoop. Each bag that lands squarely inside scores two points. Each beanbag landing on the hoop scores one point. The first player to score 15 points wins.

TOYS AND GAMES FOR A SUNNY DAY

- Badminton racket and birdie
- Balsa-wood plane
- Basketball
- Bike (with helmet)
- Bubble wand and bubbles
- Croquet
- Frisbee
- Gloves and ball (for catch)
- Hula-Hoop
- In-line skates (with helmet and knee and elbow pads)
- Kickball
- Kite
- Nerf football (for catch)
- Sidewalk chalk
- Soccer ball and goal
- Stopwatch
- Styrofoam glider plane
- Wagon
- Wiffle ball and bat

3

PLAY
WITH
OTHERS

I n the six-to-ten-year-old range, friendships become increasingly important. The way children build friendships (and learn friendship skills) is by playing with others. The more diverse the assortment of games, the more likely your child is to test different approaches to getting along with their peers. Some ideas work, while others need improvement. And so it goes in the world of learning as you play.

> Friendship skills are learned. There's no gene for them. That means you can teach them. Each month look at your child a little closer. What's the one little friendship skill that my child needs this month to be a better human being?"
>
> **—Michele Borba, EdD**
> former classroom teacher and author of
> *Parents Do Make a Difference* and *12 Simple Secrets Real Moms Know*

INDOOR PLAY

Some of the games here are silly. Some are guessing games, card games, and storytelling games that result in incredible tall tales. There are also classic play ideas that have stood the test of time, like putting on a play or creating a band. So let's celebrate friendship and fun with some of these wonderful games!

110 | FORTS AND HIDEOUTS

AGE:
6–10 years

CATEGORY:
Play with Others/
Indoor

**NUMBER OF
CHILDREN:**
Two

Watch a pile of blankets magically turn into a spaceship, a dollhouse, or a tent on the edge of the Grand Canyon.

Materials for fort building

- Blankets
- Flat or fitted bedsheets
- Tablecloths
- Large pillows
- Tables, chairs, or other furniture
- Heavy cushions or books

Materials to bring inside the fort

- Sleeping bag
- Child-safe camping gear (compass, pots and pans, water bottles)
- Maps and books
- Action figures or dolls

Play

The children drape the sheets and blankets over furniture to create a hideout or fort they can cozy up in. (Secure the sheets with

heavy cushions or books. Use tape on the sheets if needed.) Once the fort is complete, the children enter—and from there, their imaginations take over.

111 GIANT CARDBOARD BOX FORTS

Huge appliance boxes make some of the best indoor or outdoor forts for playtime with friends. Gather up one or two of these boxes before your child's playdate and you'll be amazed at how much time and imagination goes into turning this ho-hum box into something special.

A LITTLE HELP FOR THE BOSSY CHILD

Children notice when another child is bossy and always wants to run the show. If your child tends to boss her playmates around, a casual conversation behind the scenes can help her think of other ways to play. A good starting point for this conversation might be, "What would it feel like to you if Susan was always deciding what to play and bossing you around?" Then, brainstorm with your child about a plan that would allow each child to go "first" in a game or to decide what to play next, and practical ideas for sharing toys. When a playmate arrives, you might encourage the children to write a list of their three favorite things to play. Write each play idea on a little slip of paper, fold these papers in half, and drop them in a jar. The visiting playmate gets to pick a play idea from the jar first. Whenever they tire of a game, they can take turns drawing the next play idea from the jar.

LAST LAUGH

AGE:
6–10 years

CATEGORY:
Play with Others/
Indoor

**NUMBER OF
CHILDREN:**
Three or four

*Warning: This game may cause excessive
giggling in some children.*

Setup
One player volunteers to be the comic and
moves to the middle of the room; the other
players form a semicircle around him so that
everyone can see the comic's face.

Play
The comic begins making silly faces and
comical movements in silence. The other
players try their best to keep a straight face
through all the comedic actions. Every player
who laughs must move to the center and team
up with the comic to make the other players
laugh. The person who maintains a straight
face when all the other players have moved
to the middle wins. Another comic is then
selected for the next round.

113 ANIMAL STYLE
For a noisier version of the game, allow the
comic to add animal sounds to his antics.
(This version moves rather quickly, as it's
hard for the children not to laugh at the
donkey noises of a clever comic.)

SET THE STAGE FOR SUCCESSFUL PLAYDATES AT YOUR HOME

In this age range there's a fine line between setting the stage for successful playdates and micromanaging. Children can benefit from a bit of help behind the scenes to set things up or handle problems, but they also need the freedom to direct and manage their own play. Here are a few appropriate things you can do to encourage positive play with other kids at your home:

▶ Plan ahead. Have your child call a friend to set up a playdate several days in advance.

▶ Arrange playdates with a child who seems to share some interests with your own child.

▶ Prior to the playdate, ask your child which unplugged games would be most fun for the two children to play together. (Brainstorming in this way makes it less likely the children will automatically gravitate toward video games.)

▶ When children say, "We're bored," be ready with a few suggestions to help rejuvenate their play.

▶ Try to keep siblings occupied with other activities so they don't interfere with the playdate. (This is a terrific time for some one-on-one attention.)

▶ Have healthy snacks on hand. When children run and play they get hungry and tired and need to recharge. Be aware of any food allergies your child's friend may have.

▶ Supervise to ensure the children's safety, and be aware of what they are doing and where they are at all times.

▶ Get to know the parents of your child's friends. (Write down their phone numbers too.)

GRAND CANYON

AGE:
6–10 years

CATEGORY:
Play with Others/
Indoor

NUMBER OF CHILDREN:
Two to four

This is a great game to play with a group of children who are just getting to know one another.

Setup

All the children sit in a circle.

Play

One player begins the game by announcing, "I'm going to the Grand Canyon and I'm going to take _____," filling in the blank with any word that begins with the same letter as the name of the player to his right. (If her name is Mary, for example, he might say, "I'm going to the Grand Canyon and I'm going to take *mustard*.") Then the player to his right takes a turn, and so on. When each player has taken a turn, the first player announces, "I'm going to the Grand Canyon and I'm going to take _____," filling in the blank with an item beginning with the *second* letter of Mary's name (*"almonds,"* for example). The game continues with all the letters of each child's first and last names.

115 GRAND CANYON NAMES

In this more challenging version of the game, the first player lists one item for each letter of her own name in one single round of play ("I'm going to the Grand Canyon and I'm going to take *mustard*, *an apple*, *a radish*, and *yogurt*.") The next child in the circle must remember and recite everything mentioned by the previous player before going on to the items that correspond to all the letters in his first name.

DECIDING WHO GOES FIRST

Forget Shakespeare's "To be, or not to be?" When children play, it's "Who goes first?"—now that is the question! Here are some easy, no-grumbling ways to decide:

▶ Toss a coin, with one player tossing and the other calling "heads" or "tails" prior to the toss.

▶ Roll a set of dice, agreeing ahead of time that the player with the highest number goes first.

▶ The youngest player goes first!

HAYWIRE

AGE:
6–10 years

CATEGORY:
Play with Others/
Indoor

**NUMBER OF
CHILDREN:**
Three or more

*Can you make the other players go "haywire" by
saying one thing and doing another?*

Setup

One child moves to the middle of the room as
the leader; the other players form a semicircle
around her, so that everyone can see her face.

Play

The leader turns to one player and touches
one part of her own face or body while naming
another part; if she touched her chin, she
might say, "This is my eyebrow." The player
must respond by doing the reverse (touching
his eyebrow and saying, "This is my chin").
The leader tries to stump this player with five
more mixed-up messages. Players get one
point for each correct response; the leader
doesn't play for points. Each player has the
same number of turns, and the one with
the most points wins.

66

Activities are the gel for the friendship!"

—Fred Frankel, PhD
coauthor of *Friends Forever: How Parents Can Help Their Kids
Make and Keep Good Friends*

GREENGROCERIES

AGE:
6–10 years

CATEGORY:
Play with Others/
Indoor

**NUMBER OF
CHILDREN:**
Three or four

This is a fast-action guessing game using alphabet cards that can be easy or very challenging.

Materials

▸ 22 blank index cards
▸ Marker
▸ A die

Setup

Using the index cards, write one letter of the alphabet on each card, except for the letters *V, X, Y,* and *Z.* Shuffle the cards and place the deck facedown on the floor. The children sit in a circle with the die and alphabet cards in the center.

Play

One player draws an alphabet card from the deck and rolls the die. The number she rolls determines the number of grocery store items, beginning with the letter on the alphabet card, she must think of. If, for example, she draws the letter *B* and rolls the number 4, she must quickly call out four items found in a grocery store starting with the letter *B*—beans, bananas, bread, and beets. This game is fun to play without keeping score, or you can give each player one point for every item called out (the higher the number rolled, the better the chance of winning the game).

MILKSHAKE MIX-UP

AGE:
6–10 years

CATEGORY:
Play with Others/
Indoor

**NUMBER OF
CHILDREN:**
Three or more

*Here's a card game inspired by a milkshake
maker who got an eggplant confused with
blackberries.*

Materials

▸ Garden seed catalog

▸ 54 blank playing cards
(or 3-inch-by-5-inch index cards)

▸ Markers

Setup

Using a seed catalog for ideas and spelling, the
group creates 14 playing cards with the name
of a different veggie on each card: eggplant,
rutabaga, cabbage, and so on. Then the group
does the same with fruit on 26 of the blank
cards: peach, plum, date, strawberry, etc.,
repeating fruits as needed to fill out the cards.
On the remaining 14 cards, the group writes,
"Enjoy a milkshake." Shuffle the deck of cards
and place it facedown in the middle of the table.

Play

A player may have no more than four cards
at any time; fruit cards are worth one point,
and vegetable cards are worth two. When
a player gets a "milkshake" card, she must
show all her cards, receive her score, and turn
her four cards facedown in the discard pile
in the center of the table. Immediately after
discarding her hand, this player takes four

new cards from the dealer's deck to continue the game.

To begin, each player draws four cards from the deck without letting the other players see their cards. One player is chosen to start the game. If the first player has only fruit and veggie cards, he says "pass" and holds on to all four of his cards; then the player to his right proceeds in the same way, passing or showing his cards, depending on his hand.

Once everyone has either passed or shown their cards, each player must discard one card and select another from the dealer's deck in the center of the table (not to be confused with the discard pile). Once the deck of cards is depleted, shuffle the discard pile and continue playing. The first player to get 20 points wins the game. (Or you can set a timer; the player with the most points at the buzzer takes the game.)

119 MONKEYSHINES

AGE:
6–10 years

CATEGORY:
Play with Others/
Indoor

NUMBER OF CHILDREN:
Three or more

Put a few heads together and see what kind of outlandish stories you can come up with.

Materials

▶ Full-color magazines (1 for each child)

▶ Scissors

▶ Large-size basket or bowl

▶ Timer

Setup

The group cuts one photo from a magazine of a person or an animal who will become the "main character" in this progressive, collaborative story. This photo is placed faceup on the table for everyone to see. Next, each child cuts photos of 10 or more objects, such as a washing machine, car, door, shoe, baby bottle, and so on. Fold the photos in half and place them in the basket. Set the timer for 5 to 8 minutes, depending upon the number of players. Once the children get into the spirit and rhythm of quickly inventing these tall tales, you may choose to shorten or lengthen the playtime.

Play

One player begins the story by giving the main character a name and three traits or details (his age, his job, where he lives, his best friend's name). Then the opening storyteller passes the photo to the next person, who draws two "object photos" from the basket. This player invents the next few lines of this outlandish story by looking at the two items in the photos. If, for example, the items are a shoe and microwave, she might weave a tale in which the character is late for school because her shoe explodes in the microwave. Each player draws two photos from the basket and uses these items to create a progressive story of mayhem and monkeyshines. This story goes round and round, with each player adding to the story, and when the buzzer finally sounds, the player next in line pulls two photos from the basket and creates an audacious ending to the story!

120 WINNERS AND LOSERS

"We try to communicate the idea to our seven-year-old son that it's a fact of life: When you play a game, sometimes you win and sometimes you lose. And it's this way for everyone. He really likes professional baseball, so we read the scores in the paper together. He sees for himself that his favorite players have good days and bad days and their teams win sometimes and lose other times. We like to say to our son, 'The fun happens while you're playing the game, not at the end when you see who wins!'"

—Pete from Illinois

THEATRICS AND MUSIC

The marvelous thing about six-to-ten-year-olds inventing stories, puppet shows, and songs is that their emerging interests (favorite heroes, book characters, etc.) can easily be worked into the action. If, for example, your daughter is a big sports fan, she may try her hand at writing a skit called "The Night Before the Super Bowl" (see Center Stage, page 139), with her favorite quarterback becoming the main character in the plot. Or perhaps your child loved reading *Charlotte's Web*. The beloved animals in this classic can experience new adventures in your child's puppet show. If you encourage your child to follow her interests and stretch her imagination, all sorts of plots and theatrics will unfold. Here are some activities to launch your child into the magical world of at-home theatrics, storytelling, and music making.

121 STICK PUPPETS

AGE:
6–10 years

CATEGORY:
Play with Others/
Indoor

NUMBER OF CHILDREN:
Two or more

Gather up a few supplies so your child can make clever stick puppets with his friends.

Materials

▸ Wooden paint stir-sticks
▸ Markers
▸ Yarn
▸ Scraps of ribbon and fabric

Play

The children wrap ribbon and fabric scraps around the stick to create clothes and costumes. They can then attach them to the stick with tape, rubber bands, or yarn. Make a braid or wrap yarn around the top of the stick to create hair, and finish the puppet off by using markers to draw eyes, a nose, a mouth, and a mustache.

GEORGE, THE SEVEN-YEAR-OLD PLAYWRIGHT

My friend Kiki said to her son George one day, "When I was a kid, I had a friend who wrote his own play, got his friends to be the actors, and charged their parents $1.50 to come watch!" It's a funny thing how a little comment like this can launch a child into action. Indeed, George was smitten. He wrote his own story about favorite superheroes, turned it into a script, gathered friends and siblings to be the actors, assembled costumes from the dress-up box, and put props in the garage to create the set; the actors rehearsed their lines, they set up chairs for the audience, and he really, truly did charge all the parents $1.50 to watch the play. It was a memorable day for the writer and director, the actors, and the audience alike.

PUPPET STAGE

AGE:
6–10 years

CATEGORY:
Play with Others/
Indoor

**NUMBER OF
CHILDREN:**
Two or more

*A cardboard box makes quite a creative stage
for a puppet show.*

Materials

▸ Large- or medium-size cardboard box

▸ Scissors

▸ Construction paper

▸ Scotch tape

▸ Markers

▸ Puppets

▸ Assorted props

Play

Remove all four flaps from the bottom of the
box. Tuck the four top flaps into the box for
support. Turn the box on its side to create an
open "window" or stage. The children use
construction paper and tape to make a front
curtain on the box that runs along the top
and partway across each side. They can also
decorate the inside walls and floor of the
stage, and add props that go along with the
story. Set this box on the kitchen table, and
the puppeteers will crouch or kneel behind
to put on the production. They will hold the
puppets up into the air, just high enough
to see the characters, without seeing the
puppeteers' arms.

CENTER STAGE

AGE:
6–10 years

CATEGORY:
Play with Others/
Indoor

**NUMBER OF
CHILDREN:**
Two or more

Some kids will enjoy inventing a short story and ad-libbing a play on the spot, while others will string this activity over several days.

Materials

▸ Paper and pencil, for script writing

▸ Costumes and makeup, for the actors

▸ Furniture and props, for the stage

Setup

Two or more children work together to create the story for the play and turn it into a script. (One child will often take the lead, working favorite childhood stories or action heroes into the play.) Parents, siblings, grandparents, and neighbors can be invited to attend the performance; if that's the case, help the children by setting out chairs for the audience. (The children can make tickets themselves or use real tickets, available at office supply stores.)

Play

This creative venture may occur spontaneously over the course of one afternoon or be planned and stretched out over several weekends. This is a wonderful collaborative play idea for children to undertake primarily on their own. Some plays will involve one scene and two friends acting; others may be more elaborate.

LET'S PLAY BAND

Sure, lots of children six to ten years old take formal music lessons, but they *still* get a charge out of playing around with musical instruments or singing with friends. In fact, if you have kid-friendly musical instruments around, children this age are notorious for creating their own impromptu "band" for the day. Here are some kid-friendly instruments that are excellent for spontaneous jam sessions:

- Bongos
- Boomwhackers (percussion tubes)
- Steel drum, for children
- Castanets
- Child's dulcimer
- Child's guitar
- Claves
- Child's conga
- Cowbell with mallet
- Drums
- Glockenspiel

- Handbells
- Harmonica
- Kazoo
- Maracas
- Melody lap harp
- Piano or keyboard
- Recorder
- Slide whistle
- Tambourine
- Triangle
- Ukulele
- Xylophone

WORDPLAY & GUESSING GAMES

There's a whole lot of thinking going on when children six to ten play the wordplay and guessing games below. And each player brings his unique personality to the table—so be prepared for some silly antics and wild and crazy guesses. Sometimes it's a quick response that wins out, and other times mulling over the clues guarantees success. In either case, your child will discover the pleasure of using brainpower, memory, and observation skills for play.

124 ALPHABET DETECTIVE

AGE:
6–10 years

CATEGORY:
Play with Others/
Indoor

**NUMBER OF
CHILDREN:**
Two or more

What letters are missing from the alphabet? Is it the Q? Maybe the Z. Spot the missing letters quickly!

Materials

▶ 26 index cards
▶ Pencils
▶ Timer

Setup

Write one letter of the alphabet on each index card (*A* to *Z*).

Play

Shuffle the deck of cards and place the deck facedown on the ground. The first player takes three cards from the deck and, keeping them facedown, sets them aside. He sets the timer for 2 or 3 minutes and shouts, "Go!" The second player begins laying the rest of the cards faceup in a horizontal line, trying to get them back into alphabetical order so he can figure out which three letters are missing before the timer sounds. One point is scored for each correct letter guessed, for a total of three possible points per round of play. On the next round, the players switch roles. When they come to a stopping point where they've had the same number of turns, the player with the most points wins.

125 MYSTERY CIRCLE

AGE:
6–10 years

CATEGORY:
Play with Others/
Indoor

**NUMBER OF
CHILDREN:**
Two or more

This is an excellent game for mind readers (or very good friends)!

Materials

▸ Large sheets of newsprint paper
▸ Pencils

Setup

Place a sheet of paper and the pencils on the table. One child will be the Lead Artist and the other child will be the Supporting Artist.

Play

The Lead Artist thinks of a specific object or animal that could be partially represented by a circle (a bicycle, for instance). She writes the name of the object she plans to draw on a small piece of paper and, without the other artist seeing it, folds it and puts it in her pocket. The Lead Artist draws the circle on the paper and then adds two more marks, shapes, or lines to the drawing. The Supporting Artist looks at the partial drawing and silently tries to guess the object, and based upon his guess, the Supporting Artist finishes the drawing. (No speaking is allowed until the drawing is complete.) When the drawing is complete, he announces his guess aloud (in other words, he announces the finished object he has just completed). The Lead Artist takes the small, folded paper from her pocket and reads the name of the mystery object to determine if the Supporting Artist made the correct guess. This is a cooperative game, with both players working together and at times trying to stump each other.

126 NOSY PARKER

AGE:
6–10 years

CATEGORY:
Play with Others/
Indoor

**NUMBER OF
CHILDREN:**
Three or more

 TIP

Some children
will prefer a
guessing game
that features
only 12 or 24
mystery people,
so tailor this
game to your
child's abilities
and interests.

*That pile of old magazines is full of colorful
characters to use in this mystery-person
guessing game.*

Materials

▸ Full-color magazines

▸ Scissors

▸ Markers

▸ Construction paper

▸ Large paper grocery bag

Setup

Tear out 36 photos, each featuring one person,
from magazines. (Select a wide variety of
people of varying ages, looks, and clothing.)
Trim around the photos so that you focus on
one person, with little or no background. Line
these photos up on the floor, six rows across
and six rows down, creating a square. Using
a marker, write a number from 1 to 36 at the
bottom right corner of each photo. Cut 36 small
rectangles of construction paper and write
a number from 1 to 36 on each piece, folding
the pieces in half to hide the numbers. Put all
these strips of paper into the bag. Shake the
bag to mix up the numbers.

Play

The first player draws a slip of paper from the
bag and looks at the number discreetly. The
photo with the matching number represents

the "mystery person." The player to the first player's right tries to figure out the identity of the mystery person by asking questions. ("Is it a man?" "Does he have blond hair?") Once the correct picture has been identified, it is removed from the floor and set aside; the second player takes a turn drawing a number, and the player to his right takes a turn at guessing. (For a team approach to guessing, two children can alternate asking questions.) This is a fabulous game to play without keeping score, but if the children want to keep score, they can score one point for every question asked before the correct guess. The person with the least number of points wins.

GIVE YOUR CHILD A VOCABULARY TO HANDLE EMOTIONS

Sometimes when children play together, emotions flare. Frustration or anger may wash over a child like a wave, with an angry outburst putting an end to the play. Children who learn to label their feelings of frustration, anger, crankiness, or sadness are often more able to control those feelings. The child who is familiar with what frustration feels like and can use the word to describe it might be more inclined to say, "Hey, you've been using that big shovel for a long time now. Let's trade and you use this little shovel for a while."

QUIZ MASTER

AGE:
6–10 years

CATEGORY:
Play with Others/
Indoor

NUMBER OF CHILDREN:
Three or more
(with adult
assistance for
the youngest
children)

How many things can you come up with that start with the letter F?

Materials

▸ 32 blank playing cards or index cards

▸ Markers

▸ Paper and pencils for each player

▸ 1-minute egg timer (or stopwatch)

Setup

Create a card for each letter of the alphabet, omitting the letters Q, X, Y, and Z. Create another set of cards of familiar "categories" like names, sports, places, foods, books, or book characters. Select one person to be the Quiz Master. Give each child a pencil and paper. Decide in advance how many rounds to play.

Play

The Quiz Master announces the start of the game, draws one card from the category deck and one card from the letters deck, holds the cards up for everyone to see, and immediately starts the timer for one minute. The children write down as many words as possible that start with the selected letter and fall within the selected category. When the time is up, the Quiz Master looks at each child's answers; the child with the most answers wins the round and is given the alphabet card. After the first round, another child becomes the Quiz Master, and the game continues. At the end of the game, the child with the most cards wins. To play without scoring, mix the alphabet cards back in the deck of cards. In this version, a new Quiz Master is selected after five cards have been played.

GOOD THINGS CAN HAPPEN THROUGH MIXED-AGE PLAY

In the old days, neighborhood kids, siblings, and cousins of various ages played together. The younger kids intently watched the older ones in action. The older kids sometimes paused to let the little ones take a turn. This scenario was not always picture-perfect, but there was a positive benefit to mixed-age play. For one thing, the older kids had a chance to play the role of mentor, showing patience and kindness to someone smaller and less experienced. And the younger kids had access to models who were more experienced than their own peers but more accessible than grown-ups. Today, your children may have fewer opportunities built in, but on occasion you can set up mixed-age play when friends and family come to visit. If you have an older child at home and a younger child is coming to visit, ask your child to think of two or three things she can show the little one how to play.

OUTDOOR PLAY

Outdoor games provide many tremendous opportunities for building friendships and physical fitness. Children experience the thrill of running, chasing, racing, throwing, and hopping—a welcome alternative to the sitting and thinking that goes on during the school day. They learn about being on a team, playing by the rules, and being a good sport. They learn to take turns, to make amends, to take a joke, and to dust themselves off after minor mishaps and misunderstandings. And they blow off steam in a way that just can't be replicated indoors. Here are some games that mix fun, fitness, and friends.

128 OBSTACLE COURSE CROQUET

AGE:
6–10 years

CATEGORY:
Play with Others/
Outdoor

**NUMBER OF
CHILDREN:**
Two or more

Designing your own obstacle course with lawn chairs and Hula-Hoops is half the fun.

Materials
▸ Lawn chairs, basketballs, Hula-Hoops, or other safe objects to use as obstacles
▸ Welcome mat or magazines
▸ Child's (plastic) croquet set (use the mallets and balls)

Setup
The children create an obstacle course on the lawn using lawn chairs, basketballs, Hula-Hoops, old shoes, and anything else they can find. Place the welcome mat at the starting point to create "home base" and designate the last obstacle in the course as the endpoint.

They should also decide whether the croquet balls go under or around each item in the obstacle course.

Play

The first player places his croquet ball on the ground just in front of home base and uses the mallet to tap the ball toward the first item on the obstacle course. The next player places his ball at home base and takes a turn tapping a ball toward the first item. The game continues until each player has maneuvered the entire obstacle course with his croquet ball and mallet.

129 CROQUET

The traditional version of croquet is played with mallets, arches, stakes, and wooden balls on the lawn. The stakes and arches are laid out on the lawn in a particular (double-diamond) pattern. The players take turns driving their balls through each of the hoops and scoring points along the way. For children six to ten, you may wish to set up a short course and adjust the rules to suit your child's age and skill level.

FLYSWATTER VOLLEYBALL

AGE:
6–10 years

CATEGORY:
Play with Others/
Outdoor

**NUMBER OF
CHILDREN:**
Two or more

* SAFETY ALERT
Supervise all
balloon play to
prevent children
less than eight
years old from
choking on
uninflated
balloons or
balloon pieces.

*"What could you do with a flyswatter besides
swatting flies?" I asked two six-year-old boys in
my neighborhood. A wild assortment of ideas
came tumbling out.*

Materials

▸ Roll of 2-inch-wide painter's tape (or masking tape)

▸ Balloons* (or inflatable beach ball)

▸ Unused plastic flyswatters

▸ Timer

Setup

In your backyard or the park, create an
alternative volleyball net by stretching a
12-to-15-inch piece of painter's tape across
the lawn in a straight line. (Roll out about
12 inches of tape at a time, sticky side down,
on the lawn, and press it down with your feet,
section by section, to hold it firmly in place
on the grass.) Use painter's tape to create a
boundary behind each side of the net as well.

Play

Create two teams with an equal number of
players. Each team is positioned on one side
of the net. One player tosses the beach ball
into the air and swats it toward the opposite
side of the net with her flyswatter. (Players can
swat underhand or overhand.) The idea is to
keep the ball moving from one side to the other
without touching the ground. There is no limit

to the number of times a player can swat the ball to keep it in play before sending it to the other side of the net. This game can be played without keeping score, or a simple scoring system can be devised by assigning one point to a team when it fails to keep the ball in the air on its side of the net. Set the timer and play for 5 to 10 minutes; the team with the fewest points wins the round. Mix up the players to form new teams for the next round.

131 CHAOS

For eight or more players, use two beach balls, which will be swatted from player to player simultaneously. Similar rules are in effect. The object is to keep both balls in the air simultaneously, moving from player to player and side to side. (When one ball touches the ground, the nearest player simply tosses it back into the air.) This version of the game is fast-moving and can be played without keeping score.

132 FLIP-FLOP VOLLEYBALL

Use clean, adult-size flip-flops instead of flyswatters!

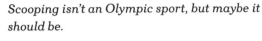

133 SCOOP-BALL

AGE:
6–10 years

CATEGORY:
Play with Others/
Outdoor

**NUMBER OF
CHILDREN:**
Two or more

Scooping isn't an Olympic sport, but maybe it should be.

Materials

▶ Large plastic pet food scoops
(1 for each child)

▶ Tennis balls or small rubber balls

Setup
Position players on the lawn a short distance away from each other.

Play
For two players, one player tosses the ball with his hand and the other player catches the ball with his scoop, or both players toss and catch the ball with the scoops (a bit more challenging). The players can increase the challenge by moving farther away from each other.

134 SCOOP-BALL RELAY
For four or more players, pair the players off in teams of two. Mark a "net line" in the middle of the lawn and line the teams up with one player on each side of the line, directly opposite his teammate. Each player has a scoop in hand, and each team gets one tennis ball. One player shouts "Scoop," and the ball is tossed from one player's scoop to his teammate's. (No hands are used in this version of the game.) Each

time a team successfully tosses and catches the ball, they score one point. When the balls have all been caught, all players take one giant step backward. The designated shouter (player) shouts "Scoop" again as the signal for the next toss to begin. (Only one toss is made by each team each time "Scoop" is called out.) The team with the most points at the end of each round wins.

135 | THREE-MINUTE WORK-IT-OUT

PARENT TIP

"My sons were having a lot of trouble working out squabbles when they played together, so I instituted the 'three-minute work-it-out-on-your-own' rule. When I overhear them arguing while they play, I'll say, 'Hey, boys, it's time for a three-minute work-it-out alone.' This is basically a signal that they need to come up with a fair way to resolve the argument or I'll come in and settle things. They know that when I settle things, sometimes they have to go to their room or the toy is put away for a few days. So they are motivated to find a friendly solution to their problem."

—Michael from Ohio

CALL-BALL

AGE:
6–10 years

CATEGORY:
Play with Others/
Outdoor

**NUMBER OF
CHILDREN:**
Three to four

*Quick reflexes are a plus in this game that
involves more than a little scrambling.*

Materials

▸ Playground ball or tennis ball

▸ Safe outdoor play area

Setup

Players form a circle around one player.
Each player in the circle is assigned a number
between 1 and 10.

Play

The player in the center throws the ball high
into the air; the moment the ball is airborne,
she calls out the number of one of the players.
The player assigned that number runs to the
center and tries to catch the ball. If she does
catch the ball, she becomes the new tosser. If
she does not catch the ball, she goes back to
the circle and the original tosser continues to
throw the ball and call numbers. (For mixed
ages or abilities, let everyone take a set number
of turns tossing the ball.) This game can also
be played by assigning the players days of the
week instead of numbers.

BEACH BLANKET TOSS

AGE:
6–10 years

CATEGORY:
Play with Others/
Outdoor

**NUMBER OF
CHILDREN:**
Two

*Send the beach ball soaring, then run in unison
to catch it.*

Materials

▸ Beach towel or king-size pillowcase
▸ Inflatable beach ball

Setup

Spread the beach towel out on the ground with
one player standing at each end. Place the
inflated beach ball in the center of the towel.

Play

Each player grabs the two corners at her end
of the beach towel or pillowcase. Players take
a step or two backward so that the cloth is
pulled tight. On the count of three, the players
jerk the towel up and send the ball into the
air. They catch the ball and work as a team,
sending the ball into the air again and running
to catch it with the towel.

"

In play, you learn how to fix the basketball hoop;
you learn how to fix the bicycle chain; you learn
how to do the math problem."

—Edward Hallowell, MD
psychiatrist and author of
Driven to Distraction and *CrazyBusy*

MONKEY IN THE MIDDLE

AGE:
6–10 years

CATEGORY:
Play with Others/
Outdoor

**NUMBER OF
CHILDREN:**
Three

Jump up and down, wave your arms in the air, add a few sound effects, and you've got a lively round of play.

Materials

▸ Playground ball

▸ Safe outdoor playing area

Setup

One child is the "monkey" and stands in the middle of the lawn; the other two players line up on opposite ends of the lawn, about 8 to 10 feet away from the monkey.

Play

The two ball tossers throw the ball back and forth across the lawn, over or around the monkey. The monkey tries to catch the ball in midair or on a bounce when a player has dropped it. The last player to touch the ball before the monkey catches it becomes the new "monkey" in the next round. (Set a time limit of 2 or 3 minutes for each monkey's turn so that nobody gets stuck out there for too long.)

WATERLOGGED

AGE:
6–10 years

CATEGORY:
Play with Others/
Outdoor

**NUMBER OF
CHILDREN:**
Two or more

A friendly game of catch using water balloons.

Materials

▸ Balloons*

▸ Water

▸ Bathing suits

▸ Plastic laundry basket

Setup

Fill balloons with water. Gently place them in the laundry basket. Position two players 3 feet apart, facing each other. With three or more players, they'll stand in a circle.

Play

One child begins a game of toss. Each time the balloon is caught, the players each take a small step backward. Replace balloons as needed.

FOUR SQUARE

AGE:
6–10 years

CATEGORY:
Play with Others/
Outdoor

**NUMBER OF
CHILDREN:**
Four or more

*Four score and seven years ago, were children
lucky enough to play this game? Let's hope so!*

Materials

▸ Chalk

▸ Blacktop or concrete playing area

▸ Playground ball

Setup

Draw a large chalk square—16-by-16-foot or
larger—on the concrete. Divide this square
into four equal-size boxes. Label the box in
the upper-left corner with the letter *A*; moving
clockwise, label the other boxes *B*, *C*, and *D*.
Select one player to start the game in square
A. The goal in this game is to spend the most
time possible in square A; the B square is
second best, C is third, and D is the least
desirable square.

Play

Each of the four players stands in one of the
lettered squares. (Any additional players stand
in a waiting line several feet away from the box;
they'll enter at the D square.) The player in the
A square bounces the ball once on the ground
and bats it underhand, using one or both hands.
She tries to bounce the ball into any other
player's square, and then that player bats the
ball into another player's square. The ball keeps
moving in this way, from square to square, until

one of the players gets an "out." A ball is out
when any of the following things happens:

▶ The ball bounces on a line.

▶ The ball bounces out of bounds.

▶ A player hits the ball overhand, or with
a closed fist, or doesn't use her hands to
bounce the ball.

▶ A player fails to hit the ball out of her box
when bouncing it to another player.

When a player in squares A, B, or C gets an
out, she moves into the D square, and each
of the other players advances into a more
favorable square to continue playing. If there
are only four players playing and the player in
the D square makes an out, she remains in the
D square. If there are players in the waiting
line, the player steps out of the square and
moves to the end of the waiting line; the first
player in the line moves into the D square.
There is no particular scoring for this game,
but the children try to stay in the A square as
long as possible.

141 PLAYGROUP FOUR SQUARE

Geared to six- and seven-year-olds who can't
master the tap and serve routine of ordinary
Four Square, this version allows the children
one bounce before they catch the ball in their
square, and rather than batting the ball they
can catch and toss it.

BEANBAG-HAT RACE

AGE:
6–10 years

CATEGORY:
Play with Others/
Outdoor

**NUMBER OF
CHILDREN:**
Four

*Do you run like the wind or take it slow and
steady? Give this game a try and discover
the answer.*

Materials

▸ Roll of 2-inch-wide painter's tape

▸ Beanbags

▸ Timer

Setup

Mark start and finish lines by placing two
6-foot-long strips of tape on the grass. (Roll
out the tape, sticky side down, in 12-inch
sections, pressing it down with your feet as
you go.)

Play

Each player lines up behind the start line with
a beanbag on his head. Announce, "Ready,
set, go!" and set the timer for 3 minutes. The
players run the race with a beanbag on their
heads. One point is scored every time a player
completes one lap of the race (start to finish
and back again). If a child drops his hat, he
must go back to the closest start or finish line
and resume racing. Keep track of the scores as
the players cross the lines.

143 BEANBAG-HAT RELAY

Divide a larger group into two teams for a relay race. The first player runs one lap with the beanbag on his head; when he reaches the start line, he hands his hat to the next player, who puts it on his own head and runs a lap. The relay continues in this manner, with the two teams running side by side.

> Physically challenged children sometimes have problems opening and closing their hands quickly enough to catch a ball. Try taking a child-size baseball glove and putting Velcro in the inside webbing. Then, put Velcro on the ball, use a batting tee, and you've got all the adaptations for throwing, catching, and batting during a five-, six-, or seven-year-old's tee ball game."
>
> **—Kristi Menear, PhD**
> professor of human studies at the
> University of Alabama at Birmingham

HOPSCOTCH

AGE:
8–10 years

CATEGORY:
Play with Others/
Outdoor

**NUMBER OF
CHILDREN:**
Two or more

*Toss, hop, and balance—a physical test of
coordination and concentration.*

Materials

▸ Chalk

▸ Sidewalk

▸ Smooth, flat stone or
bottle cap for each
player

Setup

Draw the hopscotch grid on the pavement
using chalk.

Play

Select one player to go first. This player tosses
his stone on the square marked 1. He then
jumps over this square, hopping on one foot,
taking care not to step on the lines or hop out
of bounds. The player hops on one foot on
any square that is positioned single file (the
1, 2, 3, 6, 9, and 10 squares) and may hop and
land on two feet on the squares arranged side
by side, such as the 4 and 5, and the 7 and 8
squares. On each play, when the player gets to
the number 10 square, at the end of the grid,
he must hop into that square using one foot,
turn around (without his other foot touching
the ground), and head back to the beginning
square. When he gets back to the square that is
in line immediately before the square with his
stone, he pauses, stoops down, and retrieves
the stone, and then hops back to the starting

line on each remaining square. If he has successfully hopped from one end to the other without stepping on a line, going out of bounds, or putting his other foot down when on a single file square, he takes another turn and tosses his stone onto the number 2 square and continues. Once a player fouls out, the next player takes a turn. (When the fouled-out player's turn comes around again, he starts out all over again on the numbered square that he fouled out on during his previous turn.) The game continues in this way until one player completes the entire grid and wins the game.

145 BEANBAG HOPSCOTCH

Draw a start line about 2 feet behind the first square. Using the same hopscotch grid, the children play the game by tossing a beanbag onto the numbered squares in sequence. If the first child makes his first toss into square number 1, he picks up the beanbag, returns to the start line, and aims for square number 2. When his beanbag hits the line or goes out of bounds, the second child takes a turn. When it's time for a second turn, the children start wherever they left off, aiming for the square they fouled out on. The first child to move through all the squares and land on the 10 wins the game.

146 INSIDE

If it's raining outside, stay indoors and use tape to mark the grid on the floor or carpet.

SPAGHETTI AND MEATBALLS

AGE:
6–10 years

CATEGORY:
Play with Others/
Outdoor

**NUMBER OF
CHILDREN:**
Two

*Tonight's special is flying meatballs with a side
of giggling and tumbling.*

Materials

▸ Large colander with handles
▸ Laundry basket
▸ Ping-Pong balls or newspaper balls (crumpled up
  pieces of newspaper)

Play

Both children stand in the middle of the lawn
with one child designated as the Meatball
Tosser and the other as the Catcher. (The
catcher is given the colander and the tosser
has a laundry basket full of balls.) The tosser
throws the meatballs one at a time way up into
the air, and the catcher runs to catch each ball
in her strainer. After all the balls have been
thrown, the players swap positions and play
another round.

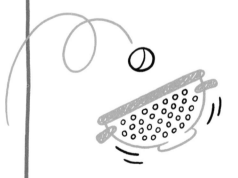

THE IMPORTANCE OF "I'M SORRY"

One of my parenting mottos is *Every child needs to learn to apologize.* I offer this in part because of the adults we have all encountered who step on the toes of others and can't bring themselves to apologize. Young children are just learning to get along with others, and they will make mistakes. The truth is, we all do from time to time, so it's important that making amends becomes an acceptable part of life. In fact, children like having something concrete they can do when they know they've been unkind. Let your kids know that they can say "I'm sorry," and that they can also *show* they are sorry with actions and kind deeds. Here are a few ways to help your child learn this important friendship skill:

▶ Be a good role model. Take responsibility when you have hurt someone's feelings or been short-tempered, and make appropriate apologies.

▶ Teach your child that if he realizes he's been unfair while playing, he can immediately say, "I'm sorry" and offer "You go first," or an extra or longer turn.

▶ Let children know it's okay to apologize later too. When your child comes home after making a mistake, let him know he can follow up with a call to the friend to say, "I was thinking about what I said (or did) and I'm sorry to have hurt your feelings (or been unfair). It won't happen again. I hope we can still be friends."

▶ Sometimes both friends have been unkind. In this case, your child can extend the olive branch by saying, "I'm sorry for my part of the argument we had today." Often, this prompts the other child to reciprocate and gives both a bridge back to friendship.

▶ Encourage your child to make amends if he has damaged or broken a friend's toy. He should use his own (allowance) money to buy a replacement toy and give it to his friend along with a short apology.

148 NET-LESS BADMINTON

AGE:
6–10 years

CATEGORY:
Play with Others/
Outdoor

**NUMBER OF
CHILDREN:**
Two or more

*Easy to learn, and those little birdies are just
so cute.*

Materials

▶ Roll of 2-inch-wide
painter's tape

▶ Badminton rackets

▶ Birdie

Setup

Mark off a large rectangular playing area
on the lawn, using tape for the boundaries.
(Roll out about 12 inches of tape at a time,
sticky side down, pressing it down with your
feet as you go to hold it firmly in place on the
grass.) Divide the court in half with another
strip of tape, creating a "net."

Play

Each player stands on one side of the net.
One player serves the birdie; he can tap it
as many times as he needs to get it over to
his opponent's side. The opponent returns
the birdie, using as many swats as necessary.
They try to keep the birdie in the air as long
as possible—no scoring necessary.

149 CLASSIC BADMINTON

In the traditional game, a net is placed in the
center of the lawn. A serving line is created
about 3 inches behind each back boundary of
the court, and the players take turns serving
and volleying the birdie, trying to keep it

airborne when it's on their own side. The serving player only scores if he is serving and his opponent drops or misses the birdie. (The server continues to serve until he makes an error—either sending the birdie out of bounds or missing a returned birdie.) When the server makes an error, the other player becomes the new server. The first player to score 21 points wins.

DECIDING WHO IS "IT"

Gather the players in a circle and have each child place both fists in the center. One child calls out the following rhyme, tapping each of the players (including herself) on one or both hands on the beat of the rhyme: "One, two, three, out goes he (or she)!" The person tapped on the last word is eliminated from the circle. The players continue with the rhyme until only one person is left in the circle. This person is "It."

Here are some other rhymes to try:

Eeny, meeny, miney, mo
Catch a tiger by the toe,
If he hollers, let him go,
Eeny, meeny, miney, mo.

One potato, two potato,
Three potato, four,
Five potato, six potato
Seven potato, more.

NOTE: See also "Deciding Who Goes First" box, page 129.

HOP, STICK, AND A JUMP

AGE:
6–10 years

CATEGORY:
Play with Others/
Outdoor

**NUMBER OF
CHILDREN:**
Two or more

*"Why don't grown-ups ever hop?" a five-year-old
boy asked his grandpa.*

Materials

▸ 12 Popsicle sticks or craft sticks
(available at art supply stores)

Setup

Place six sticks in a line on the ground about
2 feet apart. Several feet away, create a second
line of sticks parallel to the first line for a
second player.

Play

Each player stands behind her line of sticks.
On one player's "Go," the players start hopping
over each stick in their line on one foot. (If a
player loses her balance or drops her other
foot to the ground, she has to turn around
and hop back over the stick she just passed to
continue.) When a player hops over the last
stick, she switches to the other leg and hops
back to the start line, picking up the sticks as
she hops. The player who gets back to the start
line first wins.

151 RELAY HOP

Divide the players into two teams. You need six extra sticks for each team. Designate one player on each team as the stick-layer who takes charge of the extra sticks. As players hop back toward the finish line, picking up their sticks before handing off the relay to the next player, the stick-layer quickly lays down a fresh set of sticks parallel to the (vanishing) first set.

66

When a child makes a social mistake, instead of punishing the child for it, sit down with the child and do an autopsy on the situation. What went wrong? What could you have done? What options did you have? What will you do next time? And, through that kind of careful coaching, the social skills of kids can be greatly improved. It's a very, very significant job that parents have."

—Richard Lavoie, MEd
author of *It's So Much Work to Be Your Friend:
Helping the Child with Learning Disabilities Find Social Success*

HIDE-AND-SEEK

AGE:
6–10 years

CATEGORY:
Play with Others/
Outdoor

**NUMBER OF
CHILDREN:**
Three or more

What would summertime be without Hide-and-Seek—running, hiding, counting, and finding—with peepers peeping in the background and a cool breeze stirring?

Setup

Select a safe grassy area of play. One child is chosen to be "It" to start the game.

Play

"It" closes her eyes and counts to 100 while all the other players scatter about the playing area and find a place to hide. After she's done counting, "It" calls out, "Ready or not, here I come!" and goes about finding people. When she sees someone, she calls out the person's name and describes his hiding place. ("I see Peter hiding behind the palm tree next to the swing set.") Once all the players have been found, a new player is selected to be "It" and another round of play begins.

153 WITH HOME BASE

Designate out-of-bounds areas and a home base, such as a tree, lamppost, or wall. No one is allowed to hide within 50 feet of home base, however, and "It" may not hang around home base while looking for players. When "It" spots a player, she announces, "One, two, three, I see (*the player's name*)." Then "It" and the found player race for home base. If "It" gets there first, the hidden player is out for the rest of the game. If the hider gets there first, he calls out, "Home free!" and is safe. Hidden players can also sneak out of their hiding places when "It" is not looking and attempt to race to home base before being tagged or before "It" reaches home base. The game continues until everyone is caught or free. The first person who was found becomes the new "It." Or, for a less competitive version, everyone takes a turn being "It" (in alphabetical order based on first name).

66

By not overscheduling your child, you allow her to make up her own activities and fill the time; there are opportunities for dreaming, for playing, for making up things. And, ultimately, to become the kind of creative person who really makes up their own life. That's what you're doing by making sure that there's a little bit of time in every day for a child to be a child."

—T. A. Barron
author of The Lost Years series

SKIPPING ROPE

AGE:
6–10 years

CATEGORY:
Play with Others/
Outdoor

**NUMBER OF
CHILDREN:**
Three or more

NOTE

With novice
jumpers, the
children can
sing the song
and skip the
actions; more
experienced
jumpers can
imitate the
actions while
they jump.

*Introduce your child to your favorite jump rope
rhymes of yesteryear!*

Materials

▸ Jump rope (9 feet long)
▸ Sidewalk or paved playing area

Play

Two children hold the rope while one child
jumps to the rhythm of the rope. First-
time holders will need a bit of practice
synchronizing their rope twirling. See the
following variations for classic rhymes to
recite while jumping.

155 ALPHABET SONG

My name is _____ and I have a dog
named _____ .

We live in _____ and _____ likes to
eat _____ .

One jumper starts with the letter *A* and fills
in the blanks: My name is Alice, and I have
a dog named Andy, We live in Alabama and
Andy likes to eat apples. The next jumper
takes a turn and repeats the rhyme with words
starting with *B*. This jumping rhyme continues
through the letters of the alphabet and can
be easily altered to create other silly alphabet
rhymes.

156 TEDDY BEAR, TEDDY BEAR

Teddy bear, teddy bear,

Turn around.
(*turn around while jumping*)

Teddy bear, teddy bear,

Touch the ground.
(*touch the ground in between jumps*)

Teddy bear, teddy bear,

Shine your shoes.
(*bend your leg to touch hand to shoe*)

Teddy bear, teddy bear,

Read the news.
(*perform action*)

Teddy bear, teddy bear,

Go upstairs.
(*lift knees while jumping as if climbing stairs*)

Teddy bear, teddy bear,

Say your prayers.
(*perform action*)

Teddy bear, teddy bear,

Turn out the light.
(*perform action*)

Teddy bear, teddy bear,

Say good night!

157 RED-HOT PEPPER

Mabel, Mabel, set the table,

Just as fast as you are able.

Salt, sugar, vinegar, mustard . . .

And don't forget the red-hot pepper!
(*rope holders turn the rope at high speed*)

158 ONE-TWO

One, two, buckle your shoe.
(*quickly bend down and touch shoe*)

Three, four, shut the door.
(*pretend to shut door*)

Five, six, pick up sticks.
(*quickly bend and pretend to pick up sticks*)

Seven, eight, lock the gate.
(*pretend to close gate*)

Nine, ten, do it again!
(*close gate again*)

159 I LOVE COFFEE, I LOVE TEA

I love coffee, I love tea,
I want _____ to jump with me!

The jumper fills in the blank with the name of a friend he invites to jump with him. They try to jump simultaneously.

PIRATE'S MAP TREASURE HUNT

AGE:
6–10 years

CATEGORY:
Play with Others/
Outdoor

NUMBER OF CHILDREN:
Four

Arrrrrr! There's nothing a little pirate likes better than a treasure hunt.

Materials

▶ 2 shoeboxes or paper grocery bags (treasure chests)

▶ 4 apples (treasures)

▶ Newsprint paper

▶ Markers

Setup

Hide two "treasure chests" indoors or outdoors before the children arrive or while they're otherwise occupied. Try hiding one upstairs and one downstairs, or one inside and one in the backyard, so that each pair of hunters is searching for their treasure in a separate area. Create two separate map-making stations with paper and markers.

Play

Divide the four children into two pairs. Whisper one treasure location to each pair, so that each team can draw a different treasure map for the other team to follow. It works well for the children to combine a few drawn objects, like trees, bushes, or the back door, with instructions like "Take 10 giant steps, turn right, and take 30 baby steps." Suggest that each pair try to have their pirate maps finished in 20 minutes, and let the treasure hunt begin.

161 TREASURE FOR TWO

In this version for two, the children hide the treasure and draw the map, and the parent searches for the hidden treasure box.

162 STATUES

AGE:
6–10 years

CATEGORY:
Play with Others/
Outdoor

**NUMBER OF
CHILDREN:**
Three or four

The winner isn't just the person who can run the fastest, but also the person who can freeze the fastest.

Materials

▸ Roll of 2-inch-wide painter's tape

Setup

Mark a start line and finish line on the lawn by placing two 6-foot-long strips of tape on the grass. (The easiest way to do this is to roll out the tape, sticky side down, in 12-inch sections, pressing down with your feet to secure it as you go.) Select one player to be "It."

Play

All the players except "It" stand at the start line. "It" stands at the finish line with his back to the other players. After calling out, "Ready, set, go!" he loudly counts to 10; he may vary his speed, counting very fast or very slowly and changing his pace suddenly. While he counts, all his opponents run toward him to try to tag him; as soon as he stops counting, all players must freeze in their tracks like statues. "It" does a quick about-face, and anyone he catches moving is "out" and must move back to the start line and begin over again. Once "It" has been tagged, he chases all the players as they run back to the start line; if he manages to tag a player before they reach the start line, that player becomes the new "It" and the game starts over. If "It" does not manage to tag anyone, he continues to be "It." (For younger children and mixed-age play, set in place a rotation where every child takes one turn being "It" and chasing players.)

66

Parents of children with disabilities should visit the websites for the Paralympics—www.paralympic.org—and for the Special Olympics—www.specialolympics.org—to see a wide range of individuals with a variety of disabilities participating in individual and team sports. It offers the opportunity to say, 'Oh my goodness, if this person can do this, perhaps my child can too,' because unfortunately, in the general media, we don't often see pictures or news clips of individuals with disabilities being physically active."

—Kristi Menear, PhD
professor of human studies at the
University of Alabama at Birmingham

BEACH DAY

Six-to-ten-year-olds are at the prime age for soaking up all that the beach has to offer. They enjoy frolicking in the water and have the physical stamina to play all day on the shore (with sunscreen, of course), building sand castles, digging intricate tunnels, and probably making friends with the children on nearby beach blankets. Expect to spend more time in the sun than you ever thought possible, because kids in this age group will play from sunrise to sunset, and maybe beyond! And of course, supervise all beach play to ensure your child's safety.

163 SEASIDE HABITAT

AGE:
6–10 years

CATEGORY:
Play with Others/
Outdoor

**NUMBER OF
CHILDREN:**
Two or more

Playtime at the beach turns into a building extravaganza: digging canals and ponds, and making roads, bridges, and beachside dwellings of every kind!

Materials

▸ Plastic sand buckets and shovels

▸ Giant spoons and scoops

▸ Assorted plastic tubs (sherbet tubs, yogurt containers, loaf pans)

▸ Wood scraps (for bridges across the canals)

▸ Small plastic boats

Play

Create a large, shallow lake in the sand by digging with the shovels, or dig a narrow canal by scooping a 4-to-5-inch-wide trench. Angle the banks of the canal a bit so that the sides won't cave in when you add water. Fill buckets with ocean water and dump it in the lake or trench. Build homes, buildings, roads, and trees all along the edge of the lake or canal. Use wood scraps or twigs to make small bridges across the canal. Create trees along the landscape by using the Drip Castle technique (see page 180). Add boats to the water for the finishing touch.

164 GIANT CREATURES OF THE SEA

AGE:
6–10 years

CATEGORY:
Play with Others/
Outdoor

**NUMBER OF
CHILDREN:**
Two or more

Look what just crawled in—a giant, sandy sea turtle!

Materials

▸ Scoops or shovels

Play

Use scoops or shovels to create a large, round mound of sand. Turn this mound into a giant sea turtle by adding a head, legs, and a tail and drawing texture to form the shell plates. Or add more sandy mounds and shapes to create a whale, a dolphin, an octopus, a Loch Ness Monster, or other creatures of the deep.

165 DRIP CASTLE

AGE:
6–10 years

CATEGORY:
Play with Others/
Outdoor

**NUMBER OF
CHILDREN:**
Two or more

Try a neat alternative to traditional sand castle construction that requires patience, good muscle coordination, and some serious creativity.

Materials

▸ Buckets and shovels

▸ Sand castle tools

Play

Using buckets, shovels, or other sand castle tools, create sturdy sand bases for the castle walls. Then fill an empty bucket with water and add enough sand to make a wet, goopy mixture (the consistency of pancake batter). Cup your hand, dip it into the bucket, and collect a handful of watery sand. With your fingertips pointing downward, slowly let a stream of sand drip, drip, drip to form a tall, steeple-shaped turret (the pattern will resemble hot wax dripping down the side of a candle). Repeat this process to create more turrets along the top and base of the castle. You can make a whole drip-castle kingdom!

BACK-TO-BACK BEACH RUN

AGE:
8–10 years

CATEGORY:
Play with Others/
Outdoor

**NUMBER OF
CHILDREN:**
Two or more

*Lock elbows with your buddy and run up and
down the beach in this classic.*

Materials

▸ Flat, sandy stretch of beach

Setup

Use your foot (or a stick) to carve a starting
line in the sand; make a "turning line" about
50 feet down the shore. Two players stand back-
to-back at the start and lock elbows (so they are
linked at each side by their bent arms). They
position themselves so that one (the "forward
runner") faces the turning line and the other
(the "backward runner") faces backward and
will be running backward down the beach while
linked to the forward runner.

Play

The forward runner says, "Ready, set, go!" and
the two begin running down the beach, with one
player running forward and the other running
backward. (They'll learn to pace themselves so
that they can keep up without tripping.) When
the runners cross over the turning line, the
forward runner announces, "Circle round!" and
then leads the way, shuffling in a semicircular
pattern, back across the turning line in order for
the pair to run back to the start line. Once back
at the beginning, the players swap positions
before running down the beach again.

LET IT SNOW!

If you live in a part of the world that experiences all four seasons, you know that outdoor play can take on a whole new meaning in the winter. A layer of snow creates a spectacular wonderland for all sorts of play. Pull on the snow pants, zip up the coat, and pull that hat on tight! Here are a couple of classics (that require few or no props) to keep your kids busy playing for hours.

167 SNOW ANGELS

AGE:
6–10 years

CATEGORY:
Play with Others/
Outdoor

**NUMBER OF
CHILDREN:**
Two or more

I imagine kids have been making snow angels since the first blanket of snow fell on the earth.

Play

Find a fresh, untrampled layer of snow. Your child lies on his back on top of the snow, and begins moving his arms up and down and his legs together and apart (a horizontal jumping jack). When he stands up and steps out of the impression his body made in the snow, the resulting shape resembles an angel—the arm movements have become wings, and the legs, a gown. This can also be wonderful solo play (with a parent), but a group of friends can make a whole host of angels (see variation). Create a new challenge by trying to leap out of the impression while disturbing as little of the design as possible!

168 SNOW ANGEL PAPER DOLL CHAIN

When two or more kids get together to play in the snow, they can create a continuous line of snow angels that resembles a chain of cutout paper dolls strung together across a snowy lawn. The idea is for one child to create an angel in the snow and a second child to create an angel a few feet away so that the tips of the wings connect. The children continue to take turns adding more angels to create a long chain.

169 | SNOW FORTS

AGE:
6–10 years

CATEGORY:
Play with Others/
Outdoor

**NUMBER OF
CHILDREN:**
Four

A more organized form of snow play, fort building is a great group activity for an outdoor winter birthday party. It opens the door to wonderful opportunities for creative construction play.

Materials

▸ Shovels

▸ Buckets

▸ Plastic snow-block maker (optional)

Play

Allow the children to make the fort "freestyle" by packing together walls or digging tunnels. Invite them to tell you about their fort. Is it a castle? A modern ice mansion? Are there any special secrets inside? Your child will enjoy pushing snow around while building walls and designing little alcoves. All snow play should, of course, be well-supervised, as things can get slippery!

SNOW SCULPTURE

AGE:
6–10 years

CATEGORY:
Play with Others/
Outdoor

**NUMBER OF
CHILDREN:**
Four

*Let your children experiment to transform the
whole backyard into a snowy sculpture garden.*

Materials

▸ Shovels

▸ Buckets

▸ Muffin pans

▸ Plastic egg cartons

▸ Plastic spray bottle filled with water

▸ Twigs and sticks

▸ Raisins, nuts, or small stones

Play

While younger kids may stick to the traditional
snowman, the older ones may instead choose
to fashion a turtle, a dragon, a duck, or an
octopus! Or how about a snow wizard? Ski
slopes for a doll's winter break vacation?
Or try to recreate a summer sand castle.
A masterpiece can be made out of packable
wet snow using plastic shovels and buckets.
Muffin pans and plastic egg cartons from the
kitchen make great forms for mounds and
decorative additions. Use the plastic spray
bottle to add a little moisture to powdery
snow so it's more moldable. Sticks and other
underbrush can be gathered for accents
(a shaggy mane, eyebrows, the pattern on a
turtle's shell). Raisins and nuts make good
eyes and noses.

"LET'S PLAY ARMY!"

Children six to ten years old often pretend to capture or fight the enemy during their play; they seem fascinated with play scenarios pitting good versus evil, and enjoy pretending they are all-powerful and can outsmart or overpower their opponent. Some of these play themes are harmless and natural. On the other hand, sometimes war and fighting play can become truly aggressive and violent. So what's a parent to do? Here's my best advice:

▶ Talk in simple, age-appropriate ways with your child about the difference between real violence and weapons and pretend. Make your own personal values and beliefs known to your child and set clear rules to prevent play from escalating into violence.

▶ If you make the decision to not buy toy weapons of any kind, realize that your child might still turn ordinary sticks and LEGOs into pretend guns and knives from time to time to act out fantasy war play.

▶ Children are sometimes satisfied with chase, capture, and rescue games; each side has a safe zone where players can't be captured and a jail for captured opponents. Provide huge cardboard boxes and props for each home base and the children are likely to spend hours creating their base camps or hideouts.

▶ If your child is allowed to have a toy sword (with a non-blunt end) for fantasy play, set very clear rules: The sword may only hit another sword, not a playmate or any living thing. (Provide a costume box with tunics, belts, and fantasy gear for knights, kings, and queens.)

PARTY TIME!

4

PARTY
PLAY

What good things can happen when your six-to-ten-year-old plays with a large group of children at a party? He discovers that the really quiet new kid at school does the best yo-yo tricks. He learns that you have to be really patient to "wait your turn" when twelve kids are in front of you in the cake and ice cream line. He discovers that it's more fun to win, but everyone loses sometime. He makes new friends and learns new games. He learns you have to play fair and follow the rules. He discovers that he's really good at guessing riddles.

TEAM AND GROUP PLAY

Children ages six to ten typically love a good challenge. But sometimes competition creates more friction than fun. With that in mind, I designed and tested many of the games in this Party Play section with two distinct ways to play. Team Play assumes there will be two opposing teams playing, while Group Play puts all the children on one large team, racing against the timer rather than against one another. Experiment to see which version of these games suits your style and is right for the mix of children at the party.

In each of these games, the timer should be set for a specific amount of time that not only offers the group a bit of a challenge, but also allows a good chance of beating the clock. Because the number of players may vary and the distance each child must run during the relay varies too, it's best to stage a test run with your child a day or two before the party to estimate how much time might be needed for each round of play.

CREATE A PARTY PLAN

You can create an action-packed party for a group of kids with a little advance planning. Select six to eight games (or more) to keep the party moving along quickly and smoothly. And remember to improvise, allowing for a second round of play for any game that is a big hit with the children. Here is a sample party schedule:

SAMPLE PARTY ITINERARY
(2 HOURS)

OBSTACLE COURSE, page 214

FISH OUT OF WATER, page 207

MEMORY, page 189 (during cake time)

WHO AM I? page 202 (during cake time)

COLLAGE-COVERED JOURNALS, page 206

ELBOWS TO GO, page 210

TREASURE HUNT, page 222

PRICE TAG, page 192

SNEAKER SCRAMBLE, page 226

HEAVE-HO, page 212 (backup game)

INDOOR PARTY GAMES

Get your child's birthday party off to a good start by having some play activity in motion as soon as the children arrive. Have an assortment of felt-tip markers and stickers on the table so the children can personalize their own party-favor bags. The bottom line is that you need to have something nonelectronic and fun planned the moment they step inside the party arena.

171 MEMORY

AGE:
6–10 years

CATEGORY:
Party Play/
Indoor

**NUMBER OF
CHILDREN:**
Six or more

Cookie cutter, banana, keys, teddy bear, sock, spoon, stapler!

Materials

▸ Assortment of 10 to 15 small, familiar objects
▸ Cookie sheet
▸ Dish towel
▸ Paper
▸ Pencils
▸ Timer
▸ Kitchen table and chairs

Setup

Before the party begins, place 10 to 15 objects on the cookie sheet and cover it with a dish towel to keep it hidden for the time being.

Team Play

Divide the players into two teams and send each team to a different room in the house to keep them separate. (My experience has been that one team can distract the other team if they're in the same room.) Gather the children from the first team in a circle on the floor, place the cookie sheet in the middle of the circle, and remove the towel. Give the group about 20 seconds to look at the objects on the cookie sheet. When the time is up, put the towel over the cookie sheet and set it aside. Provide one player with a piece of paper and pencil and give her the task of writing down the list of objects. The group now has 2 minutes to collectively name as many objects from the tray as possible; the note taker keeps a list. At the end of the 2 minutes, uncover the tray and count up the number of correct answers on the team's list. Repeat this same game in another room with the second team, using the same tray of objects. The team that lists the most objects correctly wins. Keep each team occupied during the other team's round with a quick game of Alphabet Detective (page 141) or Smelly-Stuff (page 195). To up the challenge, you can create three separate trays of objects and have each team take three turns.

Group Play

Prepare three trays of objects and cover with dish towels. Gather the children around the kitchen table. Uncover one tray and give the

BIRTHDAY PARTY BUTTERFLIES

Sometimes a low-key conversation with a dose of brainstorming or role-playing is all that's needed to help a child who has anxiety or shyness about an upcoming birthday party he's been invited to attend.

▸ Some children may be comforted by knowing where the party is, who will be there, and how long the party will last. Provide some basic information so he can begin to get a mental picture of what this party is all about.

▸ If your child is particularly shy, help him learn two simple social skills that send a positive signal to other children: Look others in the eye when you talk to them (rather than looking at the ground), and learn to smile when you meet someone new. (The smile is a warm welcome that says, "I'm happy to meet you" or "I'd like to play with you.")

▸ If talking to others in a group setting is a problem, role-play a few things that your child might actually say to another child to break the ice. Children have their own variety of "small talk" that sends a signal of friendliness to others. Brainstorm with your child about what kids might talk about in a relaxed and friendly setting.

group 20 seconds to look at the objects. Cover the tray. Set the timer for 2 minutes and challenge the group to list every object on the tray. When the buzzer sounds, uncover the tray again to see if the team has named each object correctly. Play two more rounds with the other trays. Adjust the time as needed to give the children enough time for guessing.

PRICE TAG

AGE:
6–10 years

CATEGORY:
Party Play/
Indoor

**NUMBER OF
CHILDREN:**
Six or more

*Give the children at your child's birthday party
a chance to work on their appraisal skills.*

Materials

▶ 6 to 8 store-bought items (toy, camera, toothpaste,
hammer, wig, can of corn, etc.)

▶ Index cards

▶ Pencil

Setup

Before the party begins, place each item on
the counter or table in a long line. Fold index
cards, one for every object, in half, and stand
them up in front of each item to create "price
tags." Assign a number to each item, and
mark that number in the top corner of its price
tag. Write three possible prices on each tag,
one being the true purchase price (you can
estimate). Use your imagination, varying the
prices wildly. Create a list of the correct prices
for each item, and put this list in your pocket.

Play

The children form a long line, with the
birthday child at the head of the line. Give
each child a pencil and an index card; have
them write the numbers 1 through 8 along
the left margin of their cards so they can
write down their price guesses for each item.
Once everyone has moved through the line
of objects and written down their guesses,

read out the correct price for the first item and announce, "Raise your hand if you had this price written down for this item." (Keep a list of winners for each item.) Go through this process with each of the items; the child with the most correct guesses wins.

173 ARTIST PRICE TAG

Assemble art supplies (brushes, paints, easel, erasers, paint rollers, bucket, drawing paper, picture frame, glitter, glue, scissors, etc.) and assign each item three prices, with one being the correct selling price for the item. The player with the most correct guesses wins.

66

When kids see that they can actually go outside and play with other children and have fun, and that it's a reasonable alternative to spending all their time in front of the TV set, they might not be so resistant. I mean, if you give a kid a ball, and take him to a park to play, he might actually enjoy it."

—Henry Joseph Legere, MD
author of *Raising Healthy Eaters: 100 Tips for Parents*

TOUCHY-FEELY

AGE:
6–10 years

CATEGORY:
Party Play/
Indoor

**NUMBER OF
CHILDREN:**
Six or more

*I think it's the gross-out factor that makes
this game such a hit with six-to-ten-year-olds.
It's gooey and messy, and they like it!*

Materials

▶ Assortment of 5 objects
▶ Small ziplock bags
  (1 for each object)
▶ Paper lunch bags
▶ Cookie sheets
▶ Bandana (blindfold)
▶ Paper and pencil

Setup

Before the party, select five familiar, safe
objects that you think could be identifiable by
touch alone (cooked spaghetti, grapes, bread,
Cheerios, an eraser, a golf ball, a pack of gum,
a tube of toothpaste, a bar of soap, a hair clip,
an empty saltshaker, a necktie). Place each item
in a ziplock bag and seal it to avoid leakage.
Then place each ziplock in a paper lunch bag.
Fold the bags closed and store them on cookie
sheets until it's time to play the game.

Play

Place the paper bags in a line on the kitchen
table and bring one child into the room.
Blindfold the child and open the first paper
and ziplock bags. Place his hand inside the
ziplock bag to let him feel its contents. Allow
him 10 or more seconds to make a guess.
Repeat this touchy-feely routine with each
lunch bag, and then bring in the rest of the
children one at a time to take their turns.

(If you want to make this a competitive game, keep track with pen and paper of how many correct guesses each child makes.)

175 SMELLY-STUFF

In this version of the game, select safe, edible foods with a recognizable odor (an onion slice, a lemon, hard-boiled eggs, mustard, ketchup, cinnamon, apples, strawberries, cheese, bananas). Conceal the contents and proceed as above, but have the child smell the contents of the bag instead of feeling them.

QUICK GAMES TO KEEP THE WAITING BLUES AWAY

If you have a large group of kids waiting to take their turn, they are likely to get antsy. Set up some quick waiting games to keep them busy, with a grown-up or helper in charge. Games might include:

▸ Three Nerf balls and a laundry basket—each child tries to get all three balls in the basket.

▸ A basket of beanbags—time for some juggling practice!

▸ Plastic golf club and three Wiffle golf balls—place a Hula-Hoop on the ground 10 feet away and let each child try to send the ball inside the hoop.

▸ Disposable camera—time to experiment with some silly poses (each child makes one silly face or pose).

ORANGE PASSING RELAY

AGE:
6–10 years

CATEGORY:
Party Play/
Indoor

**NUMBER OF
CHILDREN:**
Eight or more

This game is older than your great-great-great-great grandmother, but many children today have never played it.

Materials

▸ 2 oranges (1 for each team)

▸ Timer

Team Play

Divide the players into two teams and arrange each team in a line. Give the player at the end of each line an orange. She puts the orange under her chin, and from this point forward players aren't allowed to use their hands. On your "Go," the teams pass their oranges from player to player, using only their necks and chins. If a player drops the orange, she can either pick it up with her neck and chin and pass it on *or* pick it up with her hands, in which case she must run it back to the start of the line. The first team to get the orange to the end of the line wins.

Group Play

Line up all the players in one long line and have them play against a timer.

177

ODD MAN OUT

AGE:
6–10 years

CATEGORY:
Party Play/
Indoor

NUMBER OF CHILDREN:
Six or more

Size up each opponent and make your best guess for this fast-moving guessing game.

Materials

▸ Dried beans (navy or kidney)
▸ Paper lunch bags (1 for each child)

Setup

Put 20 beans inside each bag and distribute to all players except the birthday child, who gets an empty paper bag.

Play

Line all the players up in a long line, with the birthday child at the head. With the exception of the birthday child, each player picks a small number of beans out of his paper bag, closing his fist around the beans to keep them hidden. The birthday child stops at the first player, who asks her, "Even or odd?" The birthday child must guess whether the opponent has an even or odd number of beans in his hand; then the player opens his hand to reveal the truth. If the birthday child guessed correctly, she gets to keep the beans. She travels down the line, repeating this same routine, putting any beans she wins into her own paper bag. The next player in line then moves through the line in the same way. When every player has moved through the line, count the beans; the player with the most beans wins.

MIXED-UP MESSAGE

AGE:
6–10 years

CATEGORY:
Party Play/
Indoor

**NUMBER OF
CHILDREN:**
Eight or more

*This collaborative word puzzle will have everyone
scrambling to figure out the mystery phrase
before the time is up.*

Materials

▸ Markers

▸ Construction paper

▸ Paper bag

▸ Timer

Setup

Before the party, think of a phrase with two
or three short words that would be familiar
to the children ("What's up?" "Hey, dude,"
"See ya later," "Happy birthday, Billy," etc.).
Write each letter of the phrase on a separate
sheet of construction paper and mix the pieces
up inside the bag.

Play

One child dumps all the letters on the floor,
and the group quickly (and spontaneously)
places all the letters in a horizontal line
(faceup) on the floor. One child is appointed
to be the Letter Mover. Set the timer for 1 to
3 minutes, depending upon the challenge
involved. The team members stand back
and work together to spell out the mystery
phrase. As they guess possible words, the
Letter Mover moves the letters around to form
these words. Be prepared with several bags of

"mystery letters" for extra rounds of play. If the children haven't unscrambled the message in the allotted time, you can start calling out hints.

179 MIXED-UP COLORS

Play the game with letters that spell the names of one, two, or three colors. For example, you might include letters for the words *pink*, *white*, and *blue* in a bag. (For the youngest players, choose only one color.) The group of children must quickly create the words by arranging the individual letters on the floor, announcing one color at a time as that word is assembled. (Make it known that players may not simply guess random colors without lining up the letters on the floor!) Once all the colors have been identified for that bag, the players grab another bag, dump out the letters, and begin another quick round. In this variation, set the timer for 2 to 4 minutes, so that the children can try to guess as many of the colors as possible before the buzzer sounds.

SAN DIEGO, CA

AGE:
6–10 years

CATEGORY:
Party Play/
Indoor

NUMBER OF CHILDREN:
Four or more

This game is just like Pin the Tail on the Donkey, but it starts with a map of the United States.

Materials

▶ Invisible tape
▶ Large map of the United States
▶ Marker
▶ Bandana (blindfold)
▶ Sticky tabs (from office supply store)

Setup

Use the invisible tape to hang the map at the children's eye level on a blank wall or door. Use the marker to draw a circle around San Diego, California, and point out this city to all the players before the game begins. Give each child a sticky tab.

Play

Line up the players in front of the map. Blindfold and spin the first player three times, then point her in the direction of the map. With her hands outstretched, she feels her way to the map and tries to tape her sticky tab on San Diego. Use the marker to write that child's name on the tab once it's on the map. Each child takes a turn, and the player whose sticky tab is closest to San Diego is the winner. Play additional rounds by selecting other cities on the map.

181 PIN THE TAIL ON THE DONKEY

In this traditional version of the game, you draw a large donkey on a sheet of poster board, omitting the donkey's tail. Use the marker to draw an X where the tail should be located. Cut a donkey tail out of construction paper for each player, writing each player's name on his tail; attach a large piece of invisible tape to the top of the tails so that half of the tape is sticking out. One by one each child is blindfolded, spun around three times, and pointed in the direction of the donkey drawing. The child whose tail is taped closest to the X wins the game.

> A birthday is a celebration of the life of your child. It's a day to set aside to think about where she was last year or five years ago and to reflect on her growth."
>
> **—Shelley Butler**
> coauthor of *The Field Guide to Parenting*

WHO AM I?

AGE:
6–10 years

CATEGORY:
Party Play/
Indoor

NUMBER OF CHILDREN:
Six or more

Idle time makes for trouble when you have twelve rambunctious kids sitting around the table eating birthday cake. Here's a fast-paced guessing game for entertaining the troops for ten minutes during cake and ice-cream time.

Setup

Pick a person in the children's universe, such as a teacher, a classmate, a teammate, or someone's sibling. Write down clues about this mystery person that give a small amount of information, such as, "I am a man with black hair" or "I am four years old." (It will be to your advantage to write these clues out in advance so you don't forget them once the party gets into high gear!)

Play

Recite clues about the mystery person to the children. Continue with more specific clues until the correct person is named. You could also describe sports or music figures familiar to the group of children. Start with very broad clues and keep adding more descriptive clues until someone in the group gives the correct answer.

TELEPHONE

AGE:
6–10 years

CATEGORY:
Party Play/
Indoor

**NUMBER OF
CHILDREN:**
Six or more

This game has been around for a couple of generations now, and it never fails to elicit some laughs.

Setup

The children sit on the floor in a tight circle.

Play

One child is selected to start the game. This child thinks of a serious or silly message of any kind and whispers the message clearly to the child on her left. The message might be "I left a bologna sandwich in my lunch box at school today," or something nonsensical like "My teacher ate three watermelons and a shoe for lunch today." After the first child whispers the message to her neighbor, the message is repeated from child to child around the circle. Each whisperer may say the message only once, and if the neighbor does not fully understand the message she must still pass along whatever message she believes she heard. The last child in the circle who receives the message announces it to the entire group (and it's usually quite a garbled concoction!). Once the laughter has settled down, the first whisperer announces her original message for comparison.

PERSONALIZED PARTY SHIRTS

AGE:
6–10 years

CATEGORY:
Party Play/
Indoor

**NUMBER OF
CHILDREN:**
Four or more

*Who says you need to spend an arm and a leg
to send the gang home with special keepsake
T-shirts?*

Materials

▸ Recycled tablecloth or newspapers

▸ Fabric markers or squeezable fabric paints

▸ Poster board or cardboard

▸ Plain white paper

▸ Plain white T-shirts

▸ Assorted colored pencils

Setup

Create a workstation at the kitchen table by
putting an old tablecloth or newspapers down.
Have fabric markers or paints and precut
blotters available in the center of the table,
within everyone's reach.

Create

Each child pulls her T-shirt over a large
cardboard blotter so the paint doesn't bleed
through. Give each artist a plain sheet of paper
and colored pencils so she can sketch her
design—this way she can work out the size,
color, thickness of lines, and placement of her
design on paper prior to putting paint on her
one-of-a-kind T-shirt. Once she's satisfied with

her design, she uses this sample as a guide to help lay out and create a painted masterpiece on her T-shirt. Let the paints dry, with the cardboard blotter still in place. Remove the blotter when the T-shirt is completely dry and allow each artist to model her fashion statement.

185 PERSONALIZED NIGHTSHIRTS

Use large or extra-large-size T-shirts to make Personalized Nightshirts for a sleepover party.

COLLAGE-COVERED JOURNALS

AGE:
6–10 years

CATEGORY:
Party Play/
Indoor

**NUMBER OF
CHILDREN:**
Four or more

A journal becomes even more precious when children make it from scratch.

Materials

▸ Colored computer paper

▸ Scissors

▸ Ruler

▸ Utility knife (for adult use only)

▸ Colored foam board (poster board with foam backing)

▸ Single-hole punch

▸ Yarn or thin shoelaces

▸ Markers

▸ Magazine photos and captions

▸ Nontoxic white glue

▸ Glitter

Setup

Before the party begins, cut the paper in half so that each piece is 5½ inches by 8½ inches. Use the utility knife to cut two pieces of foam board, approximately 6 inches by 9 inches. Along the left side of each piece of foam board, cut one hole (using the hole punch) 2½ inches from the bottom edge and another hole 2½ inches from the top edge. Now punch holes in your paper that line up with those in the journal covers.

Create

Each child takes a front and back journal cover and a slim stack of paper. The children assemble the journal by threading yarn or thin laces through the paper and covers and tying a knot or bow in each lace. They can decorate the front and back covers using markers, magazine photos and captions, and glitter.

OUTDOOR PARTY GAMES

When the weather is warm and dry, move the birthday crowd outside to play. Let them run, toss, and flip and flop around the backyard, or stage the party at a nearby park. These high-energy, active games are perfect for burning off a little excitement, and the party cleanup is a breeze. Here are some of my favorite relays and group games for outdoor birthday party play. There are some games in this section that require strategy and patience and others where fast thinking or physical speed win out. And always bring your sense of humor to the party—some of the props and play gear are very wacky to wear and even wackier to play with.

187 FISH OUT OF WATER

AGE:
6–10 years

CATEGORY:
Party Play/
Outdoor

**NUMBER OF
CHILDREN:**
Four or more

Last summer, I was sitting out on our dock at high tide when a big fish jumped up on the dock beside me and scared me silly. I was inspired to write this game for the neighborhood children as a way to tell the story of my visit from Mr. Mullet.

Materials

▶ Permanent marker
▶ 2 Ping-Pong balls
▶ 2 small plastic pitchers of equal size filled with water
▶ Card table or picnic table
▶ 2 medium to large buckets
▶ 2 one-cup plastic measuring cups with handle (or large plastic margarine tubs)
▶ Timer

Setup

Draw a simple fish (or write the word *fish*) on each of the Ping-Pong balls. Place one ball in each of the empty pitchers. Place these pitchers side by side on top of the picnic table or card table outside. Mark a "start line" by placing two buckets (one for each team) filled with water about 20 to 30 feet away from the picnic table. Place one plastic measuring cup on the ground next to each water bucket.

Team Play

Create two teams of players and position all the players behind their team's bucket of water. Call out "Ready, set, go!" and the first player on each team fills the measuring cup with water, hustles down to the picnic table, and dumps the water into his team's pitcher. (The players must be fast, but they must also try not to lose water along the way.) The player runs back to the starting line and gives the measuring cup to his teammate, who repeats the same routine. The players continue this relay until a cup of water causes the fish to spill out onto the ground. (Not as easy as it seems; when the pitcher is filled to the brim, the ball continues to teeter on the top.) The players on the winning team shout, "Fish Out of Water!"

Group Play

Position all the players behind the bucket of water. (Only one ball, one measuring cup, one bucket, and one pitcher are needed in this version.) Call out "Ready, set, go!" and set the timer for about 4 to 8 minutes, depending on the size of the water pitcher and the distance each player must travel with the cup of water. (Do a trial run with your child before the party and adjust the time according to the abilities of the players, allowing enough time so the group has a good chance of filling the pitcher with water before the buzzer sounds.) The game continues as above. Most kids love to play a second round to try to improve their racing time and "beat the clock."

MIX UP THE TEAMS FOR FUN AND FAIRNESS

For games that require teams, I like to continually mix up the teams after each round of play. This gives all the children an opportunity to cooperate with every member of the larger group. A simple way to make this work is to say "Rotate" after every round. This signals the first player in the line of each team to switch to the opposing team and move to the back of the line. This way no one ever feels they're unfairly stuck on a team.

188 ELBOWS TO GO

AGE:
6–10 years

CATEGORY:
Party Play/
Outdoor

**NUMBER OF
CHILDREN:**
Six or more

The grandpa at the next booth said to the waitress, "Miss, could you put my elbows in a to-go cup?" (referring to the macaroni salad on his plate). That night, driving back to our cabin, I invented this game.

Materials

▸ Roll of 2-inch-wide painter's tape

▸ 2 cookie sheets

▸ Baseball caps (1 for each child) or plastic margarine tubs (more challenging)

▸ Box of macaroni

▸ Timer

Setup

Mark start and finish lines by placing two 6-foot-long strips of tape on the ground. (The easiest way to do this is to roll out the tape, sticky side down, in 12-inch sections, pressing it down with your feet as you go to secure it.) Place the cookie sheets on the ground at the finish line with at least 3 feet of space between them.

Team Play

Divide the players into two teams, and have both teams line up behind the start line. Give each child a small plastic margarine tub or baseball cap filled with six macaroni elbows. The first player on each team puts the tub or upside-down baseball cap on his head. On your "Go," the two players run to the finish line, dump their elbows into their team's cookie sheet, and run back to the starting line. If a player drops his tub or cap during the race, he must stop to pick up the elbows and put them back in his tub or cap before continuing. The next player in line repeats this routine. The first team to finish wins.

Group Play

Use only one cookie sheet and tub or cap for this variation. Set the timer for about 4 to 8 minutes. Challenge the team to get all the players back and forth across the finish line before the buzzer sounds. Vary the time according to the number of children playing and the distance they must travel to reach the team cookie sheet. (Do a trial run with your child before the party begins to get an approximate idea of how much time is needed for each player to run the course, then allow a bit of extra time for gathering up lost macaroni!)

HEAVE-HO

AGE:
6–10 years

CATEGORY:
Party Play/
Outdoor

NUMBER OF CHILDREN:
Four or more

Here's a game that allows for a little bravado!

Materials

▶ Rope
▶ Hula-Hoop
▶ Nerf football
▶ Timer

Setup

Tie one end of the rope to the Hula-Hoop and tie the other end of the rope around a sturdy branch of a tree (this is definitely an adult task—and take care while you're up there). Position the hoop at a good tossing level for the players.

Team Play

Divide the players into two teams and position them behind the start line. The first player on one team takes a turn tossing the football through the hoop. If she is successful, she takes two giant steps backward and has another try. (Her teammates keep track of how many balls go through the hoop.) Once the player misses, the first player on the other team takes a turn, following these same rules. The game alternates back and forth, with players from each team stepping up to take a turn. Once every player has had a turn, the game is over. The team with the most points wins this round of play.

Group Play

Create two tossing lines, one a little farther from the hoop, for varying degrees of difficulty. Challenge the team to get a certain number of scores (successful tosses) in 10 minutes, and set the timer. (Set a manageable number of scores during the first round of play so that the team has a realistic chance of achieving their goal with players of mixed tossing abilities.) Each player gets two tries at tossing the football, one at each of the two tossing lines, and then the ball is quickly handed to the next player in line, who takes his two turns. The players continue to take quick tosses, with each player getting repeated turns in the 10-minute time limit. If the team is successful, increase the number of expected scores on the next round.

190 WATER–BALLOON HEAVE-HO*

* SAFETY ALERT
Supervise all balloon play to prevent children less than eight years old from choking on uninflated balloons or balloon pieces.

Play the same game as described above, but jazz things up a bit by tossing water balloons instead of a football. This game gets a lot of "oohs" and "ahs" as the water balloons break after sailing through the hoop.

OBSTACLE COURSE

AGE:
6–10 years

CATEGORY:
Party Play/
Outdoor

**NUMBER OF
CHILDREN:**
Six or more

*It's always a camp favorite, so it's such a treat
for children to be able to have their very own
obstacle course.*

Materials

▸ Wiffle golf ball, plastic
golf club, flowerpot

▸ Loops of rope or
Hula-Hoops

▸ Wooden board

▸ 3 beanbags and a bucket

▸ Backyard slide or swings

▸ Small soccer ball and goal

▸ Junior football or
Nerf football, twine,
Hula-Hoop

▸ Safety cones and
beach ball

▸ Index cards and markers

▸ Whistle

▸ Timer

Setup

Before the party begins, set up six to ten
stations using the props above. Use index
cards and markers to number each of these
stations (you might have to be creative about
where on the station to stick the card). Here
are some obstacles you might try, along with
general directions for the players:

1. Wiffle golf ball, plastic club, and flowerpot
turned on its side: Stand back and tap the
ball into the pot.

2. Loops of rope, placed in parallel lines on the
lawn: Hop from loop to loop, alternating feet.

3. Board on the ground: Walk the plank quickly
from one end to the other.

4. Three beanbags and a bucket: Stand back at the line and keep tossing until one beanbag goes into the bucket.

5. Slide or swings: Player must slide down the slide or swing back and forth three times before moving on to the next obstacle.

6. Small soccer ball and goal: Shoot the ball into the net one time.

7. Football, twine, and Hula-Hoop: Hang the hoop from a branch on the tree, throw the ball through the hoop.

8. Safety cones and beach ball: Arrange the cones in a line, with about 4 feet between cones. Players must use their feet to dribble the ball (soccer style) around each of the cones before moving on to the next obstacle.

Play

Line the players up, with the birthday child at the head of the line. Blow the whistle and start the timer. The first player begins to run through each obstacle. When he has finished the entire course, you blow the whistle to signal that it's time for the second player to take a turn. All the children complete the course as quickly as possible in an effort to beat the clock. (You might challenge them to beat last year's total team time, or your "best time" multiplied by the number of players on the team.)

SPILLIN' THE BEANS

AGE:
6–10 years

CATEGORY:
Party Play/
Outdoor

**NUMBER OF
CHILDREN:**
Six or more

*The bobbing helmets add a marvelous sense
of silliness, but there's a good dose of challenge
to this game as well.*

Materials

▶ Scissors

▶ Velcro with sticky-
back adhesive (sold at
discount or hardware
stores)

▶ Heavy-duty paper bowls
(1 for each child)

▶ Plastic headbands
(1 for each child)

▶ 2 large plastic tubs

▶ Dried navy beans or
kidney beans

▶ Timer

Setup

Cut six sets of Velcro pieces into 1-inch-long
pieces. Turn each paper bowl upside down.
Peel the tape off one of the fuzzy pieces, center
it on the bottom of the bowl, and press firmly.
Now peel the tape off one of the scratchy strips
of Velcro, center it at the top of the headband,
and press firmly. Allow the sticky tape to set
for 5 minutes. Next, attach the headband to the
bottom of the bowl by using the interlocking
Velcro.

Create a start line and finish line on the
lawn. Put two plastic tubs at the finish line.
All players put on their Spillin' the Beans
headgear. An adult is designated as Official
Bean Counter (OBC); the OBC counts out
10 beans for each player and places them in
the players' bowls.

Team Play

The OBC shouts, "Ready, set, go!" and sets the timer for 3 to 5 minutes or more. The first player on each team begins running toward the finish line (trying to spill as few beans as possible), positions his head directly over his team's tub, and carefully tips his head to spill all the beans into the tub. (Players may learn that it's best to kneel before dumping the beans.) He runs back to the starting line and tags the next player, who repeats the action. The OBC refills the bowls of players in the rear of the line as needed, since players may take a second or third turn before the timer goes off. When it sounds, the OBC counts the beans in each team's pan. The team with the most beans wins that round.

PLAY-REHEARSAL

Play a few new games with your child before a playmate arrives so he becomes comfortable with the rules and confident about playing. Then, when friends arrive, your child will have a whole repertoire of new games to play without needing you to step in with instructions.

Group Play

Decide ahead of time on the number of beans needed to win the game. The OBC puts 10 beans in each player's bowl and lines players up behind the start line; he shouts, "Ready, set, go!" and starts the timer. The players proceed as in Team Play. When the timer sounds, the OBC counts the beans in the tub to determine if the team did beat the clock *and* get the desired number of beans into the tub.

193 BEAN GRABBER

To spice things up, any player heading toward the goal can choose to stoop down and pick up spilled beans on the way—a tricky business that may prove to be more trouble than it's worth. This option may appeal to the older, more confident players in the crowd and creates an unpredictable element to the play!

194 EGG-ON-A-SPOON RELAY

AGE:
6–10 years

CATEGORY:
Party Play/
Outdoor

**NUMBER OF
CHILDREN:**
Four or more

Have a few extra hard-boiled eggs on hand—someone is sure to smash one!

CLASSIC ACTIVITY

Materials

▸ Roll of 2-inch-wide painter's tape

▸ Large gift bow (made from ribbon)

▸ Tablespoons (1 for each team)

▸ Several hard-boiled eggs in their shells (or use Ping-Pong balls for easy cleanup!)

▸ Timer

Setup

Mark start and finish lines by placing two 6-foot-long strips of tape on the ground. (The easiest way to do this is to roll out the tape in 12-inch sections, pressing down with your feet to secure it as you go.) Place the large gift bow on the ground at the finish line.

Team Play

Create two teams with an equal number of players. Line up the teams behind the start line. The first player on each team is given a spoon and a hard-boiled egg. On your "Go," the first players run to the finish line and back, balancing the egg on their spoon. (If a player drops his egg, he picks it up and goes back to the start line to begin again.) When a player touches the finish line and returns to the start line, he hands the egg and spoon to the next teammate, who repeats this same routine. The first team to have all its players successfully return to the start line wins the game.

Group Play

All the players form one team and are given this challenge: Everyone on the team must run the egg on the spoon to the finish line and back (relay style) before the buzzer sounds.

WACKY WAITER

AGE:
6–10 years

CATEGORY:
Party Play/
Outdoor

NUMBER OF CHILDREN:
Six or more

Don't dillydally—your customers are waiting! Tonight we are serving a special dish: essence of Ping-Pong ball.

Materials

▶ 1 or 2 plastic dinner plates
▶ 1 or 2 Ping-Pong balls
▶ Timer

Setup

Designate two start points and two finish points.

Team Play

Divide the players into two teams and line up each team at a start point. The first player on each team is given a large plastic dinner plate and a Ping-Pong ball. The players place the ball on their plates and, putting one or both hands under the plate, carry it waiter style to their respective finish points, running if they can and trying not to drop the ball. (If a player does drop the ball, he simply stops, picks it up, and resumes the race.) He heads back to his starting point and hands the plate to the next teammate in line. Each player runs the race, balancing the ball on the plate. The first team to have its last player return to its start point carrying the ball on the plate wins that round of play.

Group Play

Line up the team behind a single start point and start the timer. Proceed as in Team Play. The object is for all the players to run the race, carrying the platter and ball before the buzzer sounds.

196 ZIGZAG WACKY WAITER

For older players, offer a slightly more challenging game. Create two teams. Each team forms a single-file line, with the players spaced about 3 feet apart. The player at the back of each line grabs the plate and ball and, after your "Go," takes off toward the other end of the line and back again, weaving around each teammate. When he gets back to his original starting place, he hands the plate and ball to the second teammate in line. The second player begins weaving around the line of players, carrying the plate, going from one end of the line and back again. The game continues in this way until all the players have had a turn repeating this routine. The team whose last player gets back to their start place first wins the game.

TREASURE HUNT

AGE:
6–10 years

CATEGORY:
Party Play/
Outdoor

NUMBER OF CHILDREN:
Four or more

Transform your house or yard into a wonderland filled with treasure and mystery.

Materials

▸ Treasure box with prizes

▸ Pencils

▸ Paper

▸ Tape

Setup

Before the party, hide a treasure box filled with trinkets, treasures, or treats in a good hiding spot indoors or outdoors. Next, write a series of 10 to 12 progressive clues on individual pieces of paper (one clue should lead to the hiding place of the next clue). Hide each of these clues, except for the first clue, around the playing area. Consider hiding places like inside a cupboard, under the corner of an area rug, in a plastic container in the refrigerator, in a red shoe in the closet, inside an empty pitcher on the kitchen counter, or inside the pages of a favorite book on the shelf. A clue to a hiding place in the freezer might read, "Go to the coldest spot in the house." Be sure to keep a copy of all the clues in sequence on a "master clue list" that only you can review, and give hints to the children if needed.

Team Play

Create two teams and give each team its own list of treasure clues to follow, with each clue leading to a separate bag of treats or treasures. In this variation, it's best to fill both treasure boxes with exactly the same treats to keep everyone satisfied.

Group Play

Gather the group of treasure hunters together and present them with the first clue. Stick with the children throughout the treasure hunt to offer minor clues and make sure they are safe and not creating unnecessary messes. The final clue will send the group to the treasure box filled with treats. (At certain clues along the way, you can also include a very small treat for the players, like sticks of sugarless gum.)

198 MANY CLUES, MANY TREASURES

Create a list of clues, with each clue leading directly to a small hidden treasure. Give each child at the party a paper bag marked with her name containing three or four individual treasure clues on small pieces of paper. Tailor the prizes to the age and interests of each child. As the child finds a prize and puts it inside her bag, she calls out "Treasure!" before moving on to her next clue.

THREE-LEGGED RACE

AGE:
6–10 years

CATEGORY:
Party Play/
Outdoor

**NUMBER OF
CHILDREN:**
Four or more

If your child's ever wondered what life would be like as a three-legged animal, here's her chance to find out.

Materials

▸ Roll of 2-inch-wide painter's tape

▸ Large bandanas (or cloth scarves)

▸ Timer

Setup

Mark a starting line and finish line on a safe, grassy area by placing a 6-foot-long strip of tape on the ground. (The easiest way to do this is to roll out the tape, sticky side down, in 12-inch sections, pressing down with your feet to secure it as you go.) Match up two similar-size partners; each pair of partners stands side by side with their legs touching and one arm around each other's shoulders. Loosely tie a cloth scarf around the partners' ankles, binding their adjoining legs together with just enough pressure so that the scarf stays in place.

Play

On your "Go," all the partners begin running toward the finish line, cross over the line, turn, and run back to the start line. The first pair to return to the start line wins. You can also play this game as a relay race, either by dividing the children up into two teams or by playing against the clock as a group.

AGE:
6–10 years

CATEGORY:
Party Play/
Outdoor

**NUMBER OF
CHILDREN:**
Eight or more

Is that a ghost, a jumping bean, or a kangaroo?

Materials

▸ Roll of 2-inch-wide painter's tape

▸ Old pillowcases or burlap sacks (1 for each child)

Setup

Mark a start line and finish line on the lawn by placing a 6-foot-long strip of tape on the ground. Give each child a sack and line them up behind the start line. Help each child step inside her sack, showing her how to grab the top corners of the pillowcase with both hands.

Play

On your "Go," the players begin hopping toward the finish line. Once they reach the line, each child crosses over it, turns, and hops back to the starting line inside her sack. If a player falls, she must get back up, get back into the sack, and continue hopping. The first player to get back to the starting line wins. This game can also be played as a relay, either as a group or in teams.

SNEAKER SCRAMBLE

AGE:
6–10 years

CATEGORY:
Party Play/
Outdoor

**NUMBER OF
CHILDREN:**
Eight or more

Get those sneakers on and then run like the wind!

Materials

▶ Roll of 2-inch-wide painter's tape
▶ Sneakers
▶ Laundry basket
▶ Timer

Setup

Mark start and finish lines on a safe, grassy area using two 6-foot-long strips of tape. (Roll out the tape, sticky side down, in 12-inch sections, pressing down with your feet to secure it as you go.) Have all the players take off their shoes and deposit them in the laundry basket. Stir the shoes around so they are thoroughly mixed up. Place the basket at the finish line.

Team Play

Line up both teams behind the start line. On your "Go," the first player on each team runs to the pile of shoes, scrambles around to find his shoes, puts them on, ties the laces, and races back to tag the next player in line. Each player continues in the same way. The first team to have all its players wearing their own shoes wins the game.

Group Play

Line all the kids up behind the start line. Announce, "Ready, set, go!" and set the timer. All the players proceed as in Team Play. The goal is for all the players to finish the race before the buzzer sounds.

> "There is a reason why children all over the world, in every generation, forever, have tended to play the same sorts of games in the same sorts of ways with the same sorts of objects. There are always balls, there are always hoops, there are always things that look like dolls. There are always chasing and tagging and running and climbing and rolling games. The reason? The human brain has a need for it."
>
> **—Jane M. Healy, PhD**
> educational psychologist and author of
> *Your Child's Growing Mind* and *Failure to Connect: How Computers Affect Our Children's Minds*

PACK-IT-UP RELAY

AGE:
6–10 years

CATEGORY:
Party Play/
Outdoor

NUMBER OF CHILDREN:
Six or more

If your child oversleeps, there's a good chance he has had to get dressed really quickly. That skill will come in handy in this game!

Materials

▶ 10 articles of assorted clothing

▶ 2 small suitcases or tote bags

▶ Roll of 2-inch-wide painter's tape

▶ Timer

Setup

Pack five varied articles of clothing in each suitcase and shut the suitcase. Mark a start line and finish line by placing 6-foot-long strips of tape on the ground. (Roll out the tape in 12-inch sections, pressing down with your feet to secure it as you go.)

Team Play

Divide the players into two teams. Line up the teams behind the start line, and give the first player on each team a suitcase. On your "Go," the players pick up the suitcases and run to the finish line. At the finish line, they open the suitcases and put on every single item over their clothes. They must put on the items as they were intended to be worn. They then close the suitcases and dash back to the start line. Once there, they open the suitcase, take off all the clothes and pack them back up, closing the suitcase and handing it to the next teammate. This routine continues with each player. For the second round, the teams swap suitcases.

Group Play

Play as above, using only one suitcase and having the children compete against the timer. Set the timer for 4 to 8 minutes, depending on the number of players and distance they must travel during the relay. (Do a trial run with your child the day before the party, to estimate how much time is needed per child and share a few laughs as you test the game together.)

203 CARDBOARD BOX RELAY

To simplify and speed up this game, start out with each outfit in a cardboard box at the start line. The first player puts the entire outfit on, runs to the finish line and back again, takes off the outfit, and puts each item back in the box; when the last item of clothing has been dropped in the box, the second player in line repeats the same routine. The first team to complete the entire relay wins the game.

WATER PARTY GAMES

Setting up a sprinkler or hose in the backyard makes for some great freestyle splishing and splashing, slipping and sliding, but I've given the games in this section a little more structure to make way for the occasional surprise drenching—like when a water balloon bursts on the ground right at your feet. Or when a player hits a soggy home run in Water-Balloon Baseball. Expect lots of squeals and giggles, but also keep in mind that some children love group water play and others are reluctant to get wet. One thing for sure is that many of these games are good for a real soaking, so bathing suits or a change of clothes are a must. Let the water games begin!

204 SOGGY SUSAN

AGE:
6–10 years

CATEGORY:
Party Play/
Water

**NUMBER OF
CHILDREN:**
Eight or more
(plus two adults)

A wet beach towel flappin' and slippin' and drippin' while you run is silly fun for a summer day.

Materials

▶ Roll of 2-inch-wide painter's tape
▶ 2 large buckets filled with water
▶ 2 heavy-duty beach towels
▶ Bathing suits
▶ Timer

Setup

Play on a safe, grassy lawn. Mark start and finish lines by placing two 6-foot-long strips of tape on the ground. (The easiest way to do this is to roll out the tape, sticky side down,

in 12-inch sections, pressing down with your feet to secure it as you go.) Place both buckets at the finish line. Thoroughly dunk each of the beach towels in a bucket so that they are soaked to the max. You'll need two adults to continuously refill the buckets during the game.

Team Play

Hand the first player on each team a thoroughly drenched beach towel. The players wrap the towels around their waists or chests (toga style) and tuck the ends of the towel firmly in place. On your "Go," the players race to the finish line, take off the beach towels, and dunk them in the buckets of water. They then race back to the start and hand their teammates the sopping-wet towels. This routine continues until the last member of the team crosses back across the start line. Anytime a player loses the beach towel while running, he must stop, pick it up, place it back around his waist, and resume running.

Group Play

Play as in Team Play, using only one towel and bucket and having the group race against the clock.

WATER–BALLOON TOSS

AGE:
6–10 years

CATEGORY:
Party Play/
Water

**NUMBER OF
CHILDREN:**
Six or more

* **SAFETY ALERT**
Supervise all
balloon play to
prevent children
less than eight
years old from
choking on
uninflated
balloons or
balloon pieces.

Great refreshing fun on a hot-hot-hot summer day!

Materials

▸ Balloons*

▸ Water

▸ Plastic laundry basket

▸ Bathing suits

Setup

Fill a dozen or more balloons with water.
Gently place them in the laundry basket.

Play

Pair off the children. Create a line down
the center of a safe, grassy lawn; line up the
children on the line. Each set of partners
should face each other, standing about 3 feet
apart, with the line in between them. Give a
water-filled balloon to each player on the right
side of the line. On your "Go," each player
gently tosses the balloon to her partner. (It
takes finesse to toss and catch these balloons
without breaking them.) If a player's balloon
breaks, she and her partner are out of the
game during the rest of the round of play.
After each successful catch, the player who
caught the balloon takes one giant step
backward. Call out "Ready, set, go!" when
all the players are ready for the next throw,
so that all the balloon-throwing happens
simultaneously. The game continues in this
way until only one duo is left.

WATER-BALLOON BASEBALL

AGE:
6–10 years

CATEGORY:
Party Play/
Water

**NUMBER OF
CHILDREN:**
Six or more

* SAFETY ALERT
Supervise all
balloon play to
prevent children
less than eight
years old from
choking on
uninflated
balloons or
balloon pieces.

*This is an equal-opportunity activity.
Everybody gets soaked!*

Materials

▶ Balloons*
▶ Water
▶ Plastic laundry basket
▶ Foam bats

Setup

While the children put on their bathing suits,
fill up the water balloons and gently place
them in the laundry basket.

Play

This is a free-form game where one player
pitches the balloons while the other players
try to hit a home run by popping the water
balloons with the bat. (Even a "foul ball" or
"strike" makes a splash.) There are no winners
or losers in this game, just lots of fun, laughs,
and cooling off.

207 WATER-BALLOON BASKETBALL

Players take turns holding a small plastic
colander while their teammates toss water
balloons into the basket. The basket holder can
move about to assist in "catching" the balloon.

BOBBING FOR APPLES

AGE:
6–10 years

CATEGORY:
Party Play/
Water

**NUMBER OF
CHILDREN:**
Four or more

* SAFETY ALERT
Provide
continuous
adult supervision
for this game.
Set clear rules
forbidding any
player from
pushing another
player's head
into the water.

*Make like a horse and use only your teeth to grab
the shiny red apples.*

Materials

▸ Newspapers
▸ Large washtub or dishpan
▸ Apples
▸ Large towels
▸ Safety pins

Setup

Put several layers of newspapers on the floor,
then place the washtub on top of the papers
and fill it with clean, drinkable water. Float
several apples in the tub.

Play

Select one player who'll begin the game. The other players stand several feet away and may not touch or taunt this player in any way.* Create a makeshift bib for this player, using a towel and safety pin. The player kneels on the floor near the washtub, holds both hands behind her back, and attempts to grab one of the apples using only her teeth. If she is successful at biting an apple, she carefully lifts the apple out of the tub and onto the floor. Then the next player may try his luck.

LEARNING TO PLAY FAIR

Childhood is full of real-life opportunities to teach your child about playing fair. When your seven-year-old daughter comes home from school and mentions that she saw someone cheating, you have a perfect opportunity to have a chat about why cheating is wrong. When your six-year-old son sees another boy on the playground pushing the younger kids out of the way and jumping ahead on the slide, another conversation unfolds. Fairness can be explained quite simply to children: no cheating or hurting other players, giving everyone an equal turn to play, treating other players respectfully, and following the rules. Of course, parents' words and expectations about fairness are important, but children need to see their parents playing fair too.

LARGE GROUP GAMES

Getting together to play with a large group of friends offers great excitement for children six to ten. Large group games give them the chance to play many roles—each child can take a turn at chasing or fleeing, kicking or catching, leading or following. Sometimes the rules must be followed to a T; other times the children ad-lib new rules and alternate ways of playing. Here are some crowd-pleasing games that can be played competitively or just for fun.

209 CHAIN CHASE

AGE:
6–10 years

CATEGORY:
Party Play/
Large Group

**NUMBER OF
CHILDREN:**
Six or more

This game eventually melds the children into one long tagging machine.

Materials

▸ Roll of 2-inch-wide painter's tape

Setup

Create a start line by placing a 6-foot-long strip of tape on the ground. (Roll out the tape, sticky side down, in 12-inch sections, pressing down with your feet to secure it as you go.) Create a finish line 50 feet away in the same manner. Mark off sidelines to designate the out-of-bounds areas and to keep play restricted to one area of the lawn. One player is selected to be the tagger and stands between the start line and finish line. All the other players line up behind the start line.

Play

The tagger calls out, "Ready, set, run!" and all the players try to run to the finish line without being touched by the tagger. When a player is tagged, she instantly joins hands or locks elbows with the original tagger and helps tag runners on the next round of play. When all players who haven't been tagged have reached the finish line, the tagger calls out, "Ready, set, run!" again, and the players run back to the other side. Once the chain has three or more players, only the players on the end of the chain are allowed to do the tagging. The game continues until every player has been tagged. On the next round, the first person who was tagged becomes the starting tagger.

The two easiest skills to teach, which we know are the two most highly correlated traits of well-liked kids—they smile and they use eye contact. And you can reinforce both of those. 'Oh, I love that smile!' 'Oh, you were looking at your friend. He looked like he was interested in what you were saying, and you were looking like you were interested in what your friend was saying.'"

—Michele Borba, EdD
former classroom teacher and author of *Parents Do Make a Difference* and *12 Simple Secrets Real Moms Know*

BANDANA BASE

AGE:
6–10 years

CATEGORY:
Party Play/
Large Group

**NUMBER OF
CHILDREN:**
Six or more

What's your team color?

Materials

▸ 4 objects to use as bases

▸ Bucket

▸ An even number of red and blue bandanas
(1 bandana for each child)

▸ Timer

Setup

Set up one home plate and three bases on the lawn, in baseball-diamond formation, with each base about 20 feet from the next. Place the bucket near home plate.

Team Play

Form two teams. One team is given the red bandanas, and the other the blue; all the players tuck their bandanas into their side pockets or the side of their waistbands, with the edge sticking out about 3 inches. Designate one team as team 1 and the other as team 2. Set the timer for 5 minutes; on your "Go," the first player on team 1 takes off running around the bases. When she reaches home plate, she drops her bandana in the bucket and the second player begins running the bases. When this second player reaches home plate, she drops her bandana into the bucket and the third player takes off around the bases. (If the game is played with a small number of players on each team, each player must be given two or three bandanas and take two or three turns running around the bases.) The players continue running the bases and dropping bandanas into the team bucket when they return to home plate. When the buzzer sounds, count the bandanas inside the bucket to find the team's score. The timer is set for 5 minutes again, with team 2 taking a turn in exactly the same way. After each team has had their turn, the one with the most bandanas in their bucket wins.

Group Play

Play as in Team Play, using a single color of bandana, or mix them up randomly; have the group race against the clock.

211 BACKWARD BANDANA RELAY

Mark a start line and a finish line and create two teams. Place two empty buckets at the start line and give each child two or three bandanas. Set your timer for 3 to 5 minutes (depending on the number of players and distance each must run). The first player runs or quickly walks backward to the finish line and then runs normally to the start line; when he drops his bandana in the bucket, the next player on his team starts her backward jaunt. Use a timer set for a specific amount of time. When the buzzer sounds, the team with the most bandanas in their team bucket wins.

ROAMING HOOPS

AGE:
6–10 years

CATEGORY:
Party Play/
Large Group

NUMBER OF CHILDREN:
Six or more

The power of simple toys like a ball and a hoop goes way, way back in time.

Materials

▶ Roll of 2-inch-wide painter's tape
▶ Hula-Hoops
▶ Inflatable beach balls
▶ Timer

Setup

Create a free-throw line and a backboard line about 20 feet away by placing 4-to-6-foot strips of tape on the lawn sticky side down. Have the children do a test run by tossing the ball into the hoops before the game begins, to decide the best distance between the free-throw line and the backboard line. The lines should be positioned far enough apart to create a bit of a challenge, but close enough for a good shot at success.

Team Play

Form two teams and select two players from each team to be the hoops. These players stand at the backboard line, holding a large Hula-Hoop for the beach balls to pass through. The other players on the team take turns shooting beach balls from behind the free-throw line. Though the hoops start at the backboard line, they are allowed to move toward the ball in order to help get it through the hoop. Each team gets 20 shots, and the team that sinks the most baskets wins.

Group Play

Play as in Team Play, using a single hoop and having the group race against the clock.

WHAT TO DO WHEN YOUR CHILD LOSES

Elementary-age children have a natural tendency to compete with others. They are at a stage where they are trying to figure out who they are and what they're good at. Up to a point, this tendency is okay. But sometimes children get carried away and feel they must win at all times and at all costs in order to feel worthwhile; or they may feel so disappointed when they lose that they burst into tears. So what's a parent to do?

▸ Take notice of your child's many strengths and talents and be careful not to put a huge emphasis on one thing (such as her softball abilities).

▸ Help your child develop an attitude of fair play and learn what it means to be a good sport.

▸ Encourage your child to do his personal best, to go for practice and improvement rather than being better than everyone else.

▸ Listen attentively when your child expresses disappointment about losing, and let her know that everyone loses sometimes.

KICKBALL

CATEGORY:
Party Play/
Large Group

NUMBER OF CHILDREN:
Eleven to twenty

NOTE

Since this is a game with fairly complex rules, be flexible and improvise as you see how children respond.

This old-time favorite is tailor-made for kids, but grown-ups seem to like it too!

Materials

▶ Squares of carpet or bath mats

▶ Playground ball

Setup

Create a baseball diamond in the lawn, with home plate, a pitcher's mound, and first, second, and third bases. For older kids, place the bases 30 feet apart; halve that distance for younger kids. Divide the children into two teams.

Play

Toss a coin to see which team goes first. The team in the field disperses players at each base and in the outfield. The team at bat lines its players up to establish a kicking order. (Every player gets a turn before anyone can kick a second time.)

The team in the field chooses from the following four positions: the *pitcher* stands at the pitcher's mound and rolls the ball to the kicker; the *catcher* stands behind the kicker at home plate, trying to catch the ball and get the player out; the *base players* are positioned at each of the three bases to try to catch the balls, kicking them to whichever base the kicker is approaching to get him out; and the *outfielders* stand farther out and perform the same role as the base players.

Once everyone is in place, the pitcher rolls the ball to the first kicker. When she kicks the ball into the field, she runs the bases. The batting team scores a point for every player who runs home. Additional rules follow:

Strikes

If the kicker attempts to kick the ball but misses it, this is a strike. If the ball is kicked outside the foul line (the line that runs from home plate to first base and home plate to third base), the kicker receives a strike. Three strikes (of any kind) and the kicker is out.

Balls

If the pitcher rolls the ball high or way off course, his pitch counts as a ball. Four balls means the kicker gets to walk to first base, any player on first moves to second base, and so on.

Outs

If a player on the field catches a ball before it hits the ground or tags a base before the kicker gets there and while the kicker is still between bases, the kicker is out.

If the kicker gets tagged (touched lightly) by the ball while running to a base, he is out. Any other player running between bases can also be tagged by the ball.

After three outs, the inning is over, and the teams switch places and roles.

Steals

Players on any base may attempt to run to the next base as soon as the pitcher rolls the ball to the kicker, but before she actually kicks it. However, if this stealer is tagged by the ball in the process, he is out.

Runs

One point is scored for every player who runs to home base on any play.

Innings

Traditionally there are nine innings in the game, but shorten the game to only a few innings and mix up the teams if you like to keep younger children interested.

> As an adult at a party, when you want to be involved in a conversation, you just don't go up and say, 'What are you talking about? Can I talk?' You listen to the conversation, you figure out what people are talking about, and you say something that's relevant. Young kids have to learn this same sort of thing. To a certain extent you have to adapt to the group rather than the group adapting to you. If we give children the opportunity to learn these kinds of entry skills and learn how to share, they'll be much more successful than if we do the intervention for them."
>
> **—William Corsaro, PhD**
> author of *We're Friends, Right?: Inside Kids' Culture*

DRAGON'S TAIL

AGE:
5–8 years

CATEGORY:
Party Play/
Large Group

**NUMBER OF
CHILDREN:**
Eight or more

This dragon doesn't breathe fire, but it sure doesn't like it when you pull its tail!

Materials

▶ 2 bandanas or small scarves

▶ Timer

▶ Paper

▶ Pencil

Setup

Form two teams; each team creates a dragon by lining up, facing the same direction, and holding on to the waist of the player in front of him. The player at the end of each dragon tucks a bandana in his back pocket or into the back of his waistband, leaving the end dangling so that the tail is hanging out. Players then decide upon the in-bounds and out-of-bounds areas for this chasing game.

Play

Begin with each team at opposite ends of the yard. Set the timer for 8 to 10 minutes, and as one player calls out, "Dragon's Tail," both teams run toward the center. Now the dragons try to steal each other's tails! The first player in line is the only player allowed to try to do this. Each time a team successfully yanks the other's tail, it scores a point. Keep track of the points so the players can concentrate on the task at hand.

CAPTURE THE FLAG

AGE:
6–10 years

CATEGORY:
Party Play/
Large Group

**NUMBER OF
CHILDREN:**
Eight or more

*With its multiple choices and fast-moving action,
Capture the Flag is both tactical and athletic.*

Materials

▸ Roll of 2-inch-wide painter's tape
▸ Bandanas in 2 different colors (1 for each child)
▸ Timer (optional)

Setup

Divide the children into two teams and assign each team a bandana color. Create a square playing area and mark a line down the center by placing a length of tape on the lawn, sticky side down. Assign each team to a half. All players place their bandanas on the ground along their back boundary and stand slightly in front of them.

Play

On your "Go," each team rushes toward the other team's end of the field, trying to capture their opponent's "flag" (bandana) and carry it to their own end of the field. If a player is tagged on the opposing team's field before she has successfully captured a flag, she is considered captured. Once captured, she must stand behind her opponents' flags until one of her own teammates manages to cross over and tag her, setting her free. (So tagging is an action with two uses in this game: You can tag a captured member of your own team to set her free, or you can tag an opponent to imprison him.) If a player is successful in grabbing an opponent's flag, he runs back to his own side of the field and cannot be tagged along the way. (But players can only capture one flag at a time and can't capture a flag and free a teammate in the same run.) The team that captures all its opponent's flags wins the game; or set a timer for 10 minutes, and the team with the most flags at the sound of the buzzer wins the round.

TEN-MINUTE CLEANUP RULE

Whether they're playing bandana relays, building forts, or putting on puppet shows, kids having all that fabulous fun usually leave a mess in their wake. Let your kids (and their playmates) know in advance that they need to allow for ten minutes of cleanup time at the end of playtime. You might even want to talk to the other parents in your child's group of friends and try to get everyone to set this house rule in place. When everyone is on the same page about this rule, children come to expect and respect this cleanup responsibility.

RED ROVER

AGE:
6–10 years

CATEGORY:
Party Play/
Large Group

**NUMBER OF
CHILDREN:**
Eight or more

This game gives the players a chance to see how strong they can be when they combine muscle power with strategy.

Materials

▸ Timer

Setup

Create two teams and have them each select a team captain. One team lines up at one end of the lawn with all team members holding hands tightly; the other team lines up facing the first team at the other end of the lawn. Allow some extra room behind each team line for space to run. Set the timer for 10 to 15 minutes.

Play

The captain of the first team picks one member of the second team and extends her this invitation: "Red Rover, Red Rover, let _____ come over" (*insert the player's name*). The selected player runs toward the line of opposing players and attempts to break through their hands. If he is successful, he picks one opponent from the line (other than the captain) to join his own team at the other end of the field. If the charging player is not successful at breaking through the line, then he becomes a member of the team that caught him. Then it's the second team's turn to call Red Rover, and each team continues taking turns. When the buzzer sounds, the team with the most players takes the round.

FAMILY GAME NIGHT

One first-rate way to vote *yes* for family playtime is to create a Family Game Night that both parents and children can count on. Put it on your calendar, once a month or once a week, and make a commitment to this family tradition. (Yes, even during the teen years.) Of course, what you do together will change as the children move through each stage of their development, but the main ingredients remain the same—fun, play, and time together!

WHAT GOES ON AT FAMILY GAME NIGHT?

Here are a few words of wisdom to make your Family Game Night successful and exciting. Start with some easy foods like pizza or sandwiches eaten picnic style on a blanket on the floor, or decide to have breakfast for dinner. Set aside two hours for the event, and select a variety of games. (Nearly everyone will get bored with ninety minutes of playing one board game.) You may find it best to play two short, silly games that require a bit of moving around, followed by a guessing game or two. Then move on to twenty minutes of a truly engaging board game. (I've listed my favorites on the following pages.) Create your personalized Family Game Night to suit your family's style, interests, ages, and individual personalities. So, without further ado, here are the best games in this book for family playtime.

GAMES THAT REQUIRE MOVING ABOUT INDOORS

To get everyone engaged and their energy up, a few active games are just the thing. Pick a few to try, taking into consideration the age range of the children playing, and then move on to a game around the kitchen table.

▸ Beanbag Horseshoes (ages 3-10), page 120

▸ Elbows to Go (ages 6-10), page 210

▸ Last Laugh (ages 3-10), page 126

▸ Orange Passing Relay (ages 6-10), page 196

GAMES PLAYED AT THE KITCHEN TABLE

The kitchen table is a bustling center of family activity, and why should it stop after the last dish is cleared after dinner? Save the dishes for later—it's time to play!

▸ Alphabet Garden (ages 6-10), page 42

▸ Blind Sketching (ages 6-10), page 41

▸ Concentration (ages 3-10), page 88

▸ Desert Island (ages 3-10), page 92

▸ Dictionary Detective (ages 6-10), page 102

▸ Did You Know? (ages 3-10), page 94

▸ Dog Diaries (ages 3-10), page 44

▸ Draw Me a Story (ages 6-10), page 43

▸ Family Favorites (ages 3-10), page 92

▸ Going on a Picnic (ages 6-10), page 87

▸ Grand Canyon (ages 6-10), page 128

▸ I Spy (ages 3-10), page 96

▸ I'm Thinking of a Food . . . (ages 3-10), page 103

▸ Memory (ages 6-10), page 189

▸ Odd Man Out (ages 6-10), page 197

▸ Quiz Master (ages 6-10), page 146

▸ Rhyming Riddles (ages 5-10), page 86

▶ Tall Tales
(ages 6–10),
page 46

▶ Ten-in-Thirty
(ages 6–10),
page 39

▶ What's That
You're Eating?
(ages 3–10),
page 97

Classic Board Games for Family Game Night

▶ Animal Rummy
card game
(ages 4+)

▶ Backgammon
(ages 6+)

▶ Bingo
(ages 6+)

▶ Boggle Jr.
(ages 3+)

▶ Cadoo
(ages 7+)

▶ Candy Land
(ages 3+)

▶ Checkers
(ages 6+)

▶ Chess
(ages 6+)

▶ Chinese Checkers
(ages 6+)

▶ Chutes and
Ladders
(ages 3+)

▶ Clue (ages 8+),
Clue Jr. (ages 5+)

▶ Connect Four
(ages 7+)

▶ Cootie
(ages 3+)

▶ Dominoes
(ages 6+)

▶ Go Fish
(ages 4+)

▶ Goodnight
Moon Game
(ages 3+)

▶ Guess Who?
(ages 6+)

▶ Hi Ho! Cherry-O
(ages 3+)

▶ Honey Bee
Tree Game
(ages 3+)

▶ Hungry Hungry
Hippos (ages 4+)

▶ I Spy Preschool
Game (ages 3+)

▶ Jenga (ages 5+)

▶ Ker Plunk
(ages 5+)

▶ Mancala
(ages 6+)

▶ Marbles
(ages 6+)

▶ Memory Game
(ages 4+)

▶ Monopoly
(ages 8+) and
Monopoly Junior
(ages 5–8)

▶ Mouse Trap
(ages 6+)

▶ Mr. Mouth
(ages 5+)

▶ Parcheesi
(ages 6+)

▶ Pick-up Sticks
(ages 6+)

▶ Pitt (ages 8+)

▶ Preschool Bingo
(ages 4+)

▶ Scrabble
(ages 8+)

▶ Scrabble Junior
(ages 5+)

▶ Sorry!
(ages 6+)

▶ Spill and Spell
(ages 8+)

▶ Trouble
(ages 5+)

▶ Uno (ages 7+)

▶ Yahtzee
(ages 8+)

GAMES FOR OUTDOORS

When the weather outside is warm (and far from frightful), here are a few suggestions for outside play that the whole family can get in on.

▸ Beanbag Horseshoes (ages 6–10), page 120

▸ Beanbag Target Toss (ages 6–10), page 82

▸ Call-Ball (ages 6–10), page 154

▸ Croquet (ages 6–10), page 149

▸ Flyswatter Volleyball (ages 6–10), page 150

▸ Frisbee

▸ Horse (ages 6–10), page 119

▸ Horseshoes

▸ Kickball (ages 8–10), page 242

▸ Kite flying

▸ Nerf football

▸ Net-less Badminton (ages 6–10), page 166

▸ A Real Scavenger (ages 6–10), page 79

▸ Three- or Four-Way Catch

BEAT THE BOREDOM BLUES

Create a Challenge Jar by filling a jar with small slips of paper with creative play challenges. When your child says "I'm bored," open the jar, have your child pull out a play challenge, and let the fun begin. Fill the jar with interesting ideas that test your child's thinking skills or memory, imagination, or physical stamina. Create challenges that will appeal to your child's interests and abilities. Here are a few ideas to get your creative juices flowing. (You may increase interest in these games if you set the timer for a specific amount of time allowed to complete each challenge.)

▸ Write down the names of all the professional athletes you can think of.

▸ Think of as many places, names, and foods as possible that begin with the letter _____. (Throw some Scrabble letters into the jar.)

▸ Build three LEGO buildings before the timer goes off.

▸ Complete three puzzles in twenty minutes.

THE WELL-STOCKED GRADE SCHOOL TOY CUPBOARD

FOR FREESTYLE PLAY

- Action figures
- Balloons*
- Beanbags
- Blocks (wooden, cardboard, plastic)
- Dolls, dollhouse, and accessories
- Dress-up clothes
- Gyroscope
- Jacks
- LEGOs and construction toys
- Miniature cars and ramps
- Models (planes, spaceships, boats, cars)
- Pick-up sticks
- Playing cards
- Puppets
- Puzzles
- Safe hand tools, tool belt, and toolbox
- Stuffed animals
- Yo-yo

FOR OUTDOOR PLAY

- Backyard swing set and/or slide
- Badminton racket and birdie
- Balsa wood plane
- Baseball glove and ball
- Basketball and hoop (adjustable)
- Bicycle (and helmet)
- Child-size (or toy) golf clubs and tees
- Croquet
- Frisbee
- Giant bubble wand and bubbles
- Giant Styrofoam glider (plane)
- Hula-Hoop
- Inflatable beach ball
- In-line skates (with helmet, knee, and elbow pads)
- Jump rope
- Kickball croquet
- Kites
- Nerf (soft) baseball and bat
- Nerf football
- Ping-Pong balls
- Plastic snow-block mold
- Playground ball
- Rubber balls
- Sand and beach toys
- Sidewalk chalk
- Soccer ball and goal
- Sports cones
- Swings and climbing gym
- Tennis balls

- ▸ Tetherball
- ▸ Volleyball
- ▸ Wagon
- ▸ Water and squirt toys
- ▸ Water balloons*
- ▸ Wiffle ball and bat

*Safety Alert: Supervise all balloon play to prevent children less than eight years old from choking on uninflated balloons or balloon pieces.

HOUSEHOLD ITEMS

- ▸ Bandanas and scarves
- ▸ Bath mats or carpet squares
- ▸ Bedding (blankets, bedsheets, sleeping bags, pillowcases, and pillows)
- ▸ Books (cookbooks, travel books, baby name books)
- ▸ Bowls (unbreakable)
- ▸ Buckets (plastic and/ or metal galvanized)
- ▸ Buttons
- ▸ Camping supplies (compass, canteen, etc.)
- ▸ Cardboard boxes and shoeboxes
- ▸ Colander (large)
- ▸ Cooler (small)
- ▸ Dice
- ▸ Dry grains and legumes (beans, rice, lentils)

- ▸ Envelopes
- ▸ Flip-flops
- ▸ Flower pots (empty)
- ▸ Flyswatter (new)
- ▸ Food stuffs (apples, oranges, peanuts in the shell, hard-boiled eggs, dry pasta)
- ▸ Funnel
- ▸ Grocery bags (plastic, paper, cloth)
- ▸ Kitchen utensils (pots, pans, muffin tins, cookie sheets, pie pans, pitchers, measuring cups and spoons)
- ▸ Laundry basket (plastic)
- ▸ Office supplies (notepads, pens, sticky notes, paper clips)
- ▸ Paper cups, bowls, towels, plates

- ▸ Photos of family and friends
- ▸ Plastic containers (margarine tubs, yogurt cartons, Tupperware)
- ▸ Plastic headbands
- ▸ Plastic kitchenware (utensils, cups, plates)
- ▸ Plastic pet-food scoops
- ▸ Roll of tickets
- ▸ Rope or twine
- ▸ Sheets and tablecloths
- ▸ Shoelaces (new)
- ▸ Shovels, large scoops, and spoons (plastic and child-friendly)
- ▸ Spray bottles
- ▸ Suitcases
- ▸ Tape (duct, invisible, packing, masking, and painter's)

- Timers (egg timer, kitchen timer, stopwatch)
- Towels (dish, beach, bath, washcloth)
- Utility knife (for adult use only)
- Whistle
- Wooden boards or planks
- Yardstick and/or ruler

FOR ARTS AND CRAFTS

- Artist's easel
- Artist's portfolio
- Artist's smock
- Blank journal and/or sketchbook
- Cardboard boxes
- Colored pencils
- Construction paper
- Crayons
- Crepe paper or streamers
- Eyedroppers
- Fabric
- Fine-tipped markers, washable markers, fabric markers
- Foam board, cardboard, matte board, poster board
- Glitter
- Glue (nontoxic)
- Index cards
- Kneaded eraser
- Lunch bags
- Magazines with color photos (catalogs, fliers, pamphlets)
- Modeling clay
- Needle and thread
- Paintbrushes (assorted)
- Paint roller and pan
- Paints (nontoxic, washable)
- Paper (sketch, newsprint, butcher, printer, drawing)
- Pastel chalk
- Pencils
- Play dough
- Safety pins
- Scissors
- Shoeboxes
- Single-hole punch
- Sponges and/or Sponge 'Ums
- String, yarn, rawhide laces, dental floss, and ribbon
- Tempera paints and fabric paints
- T-shirts (adult- and child-size)
- Velcro

FOR MUSIC

- Bells
- Bongos
- Boomwhackers (percussion tubes)
- Calypso steel drum (child-size)
- Castanets
- Claves
- Conga (child-size)
- Cowbell with mallet
- Drums
- Dulcimer (child-size)
- Glockenspiel
- Guitar (child-size)
- Handbells
- Harmonica
- Kazoos
- Maracas
- Melody lap harp
- Musical shakers
- Piano or keyboard
- Recorder (wind instrument)
- Slide whistle
- Tambourine
- Ukulele
- Xylophone

Two of my favorite sources for musical instruments for young children who want to experiment with music are Groth Music (www.grothmusic.com) and Music123 (www.music123.com).

Musical Play Props

The only electronic gear mentioned in this book, these props provide music for many classic movement games.

- Music and music player

BOARD AND CARD GAMES

- Backgammon
- Bingo
- Checkers
- Chess
- Chinese Checkers
- Chutes and Ladders
- Clue, Clue Jr.
- Connect Four
- Crazy Eights
- Dominoes
- Great States Game
- Guess Who?
- Ker Plunk
- Mancala
- Marbles
- Monopoly, Monopoly Junior
- Mouse Trap
- Mr. Mouth
- Parcheesi
- Pick-up Sticks
- Pitt
- Rush Hour, Rush Hour Junior
- Scrabble, Scrabble Junior
- Sorry!
- Spill and Spell
- Topple Game
- Twister
- Uno
- Yahtzee

INDEX

ACKNOWLEDGMENTS

This book is built upon the play experiences of real children who have engaged in all sorts of creative, active play. Let me begin by thanking my own children, Cassidy, Olivia, and Peter, for being such enthusiastic unplugged players during every stage of their childhood. Their exuberant, clever play ideas are woven into each section of this book.

I am deeply indebted to the fabulous game brainstormer and play reviewer (and extraordinary mom) Kiki Walker. Her marvelous can-do attitude made the research phase of this book a delightful experience.

Thank you also to the following children and parents who provided play ideas and tested games: Lakeshia Alexander; Carol Brown; Tom Daldin; John, Molli, Samantha, and Patricia Dowd; Jonnie, Bud, Andrew, Christian, Joanna, and Mary Grace Furmanchik; Anne, Ed, Claire, and Sam Gutshall; Ann Jenkins; Virginia McCann; Fulton and Ren Millis; Rob, Susan, Teddy, Julia, and Daniel Monyak; Christina, Chris, Jack, Kate, and Lucy Oxford; Liz and Bob Sauntry; Duncan, Lisa, Will, and Catherine Sherer; Els Sincebaugh; Breonna Tiller; Jacob Ufkes; Doug, Jack, George, Harry, and Lucy Walker; and Debbie Willis. Olivia Conner's creative thinking skills and artistic talents helped shape many of the arts and crafts projects in the book.

In my professional life, I have had the great pleasure of interviewing hundreds of wise and compassionate child development specialists about play, friendships, growing, and learning in my twenty-one years as host of *The Parent's Journal* public radio show. I offer a special thanks to these childhood experts, who have generously shared their insight, words of wisdom, and interview quotes in this book. (Julia Vanderelst stayed busy typing hundreds of hours of program transcripts from *The Parent's Journal* to capture these quotes.) Also, I could not have written this book without the dedication of my radio coworkers: Ellen Pruitt, Bruce Roberts, and Madeleine Thomas.

My first-rate agent (and terrific human being), Jim Levine, found just the right publisher for my book. Nina Graybill wears two hats marvelously well—both talented writer and outstanding attorney—and her advice and suggestions are much appreciated.

The exceptional team at Workman has made the publishing of this book a wonderful, collaborative experience. In the beginning, Peter Workman gave his enthusiastic "yes" to the importance of unplugged play. Megan Nicolay and Rachael Mt. Pleasant have been outstanding editors and delights to work with, providing creative ideas, careful editing, and great attention to detail. Suzie Bolotin nurtured this book from start to finish, offering a brilliant combination of encouragement, review, and fine editing along the way. The splendid art, illustrations, typesetting, and design provided by Bart Aalbers, Barbara Peragine, and Rae Ann Spitzenberger capture the essence of children at play and provide an easy-to-navigate format. Others at Workman I especially wish to thank are Angie Chen, Doug Wolff, Abigail Sokolsky, and Claire Gross. It has been a great pleasure to work with each and every one of you.

ABOUT THE AUTHOR

Bobbi Conner was the creator, producer, and host of the nationally syndicated public radio program *The Parent's Journal* for more than twenty years. She is the author of six books for parents and children, including *Everyday Opportunities for Extraordinary Parenting*, *The Book of Birthday Letters*, and *The Giant Book of Creativity for Kids*. She lives in Charleston, South Carolina.